COCKTAIL COOKBOOK

Quarto is the authority on a wide range of topics.

Quarto educates, entertains and enriches the lives of our readers – enthusiasts and lovers of hands-on living.

www.QuartoKnows.com

Frances Lincoln Limited
A subsidiary of Quarto Publishing Group UK
74–77 White Lion Street
London N1 9PF

Cocktail Cookbook
Copyright © Frances Lincoln Ltd 2016
Text © Oskar Kinberg 2016
Photographs © Joakim Blockström 2016
Design: Glenn Howard
Commissioning editor: Zena Alkayat

First Frances Lincoln edition 2016

A catalogue record for this book is available from the British Library.

ISBN 978-0-7112-3828-2

Printed and bound in China

2 3 4 5 6 7 8 9

COCKTAIL COOKBOOK

OSKAR KINBERG

CONTENTS

MEET THE MAKER

I told my friend I was writing a book, he asked me what about. I said my memoirs. We both laughed...

Let's start where it gets relevant.

I moved to London from Linköping in Sweden when I was 20 with money the Swedish government paid me for my services in the army. I came here knowing I wasn't ready for university, responsibility or any grown-up stuff. I wanted to have fun. My friend suggested we should do a bartender course and then work as bartenders. I had seen the softcore motion picture that is Cocktail, I already had a fascination for booze and I didn't mind too much being the centre of attention. This all sounded great! I fell in love straight away. When I did my first shift I never wanted it to finish. There was this satisfaction about making drinks in a busy environment. And getting paid to party! The more I learned the more I enjoyed it. A busy shift becomes a well-rehearsed dance. You know exactly where every bottle is, how much is in it, how it will bubble, what angle gives you the perfect pour, who's next in line, your left hand doing one thing while the right is doing something else: perfect harmony in a chaotic environment.

In the beginning I kept telling myself I would do a year max and then move back to Sweden.

I had a lot of fun in that first year and it became another one, then another one. It got *really* fun and interesting when I started working at The Cuckoo Club. That is where I realised I could do this for the rest of my life and, initially unknowingly, where I met my future business partner Ollie Dabbous.

There are a few people that have influenced me in my bartending career. First it was Vince Silva, who in the month-long course at the London Bar School did his best to teach me to look cool while pouring and shaking. Not an easy task. In my first nightclub job at Mo*Vida I was working for Mark Fairweather. He taught me the importance of speed and efficiency and customer service, he treated me to my first plate of sushi (in Nobu, wearing a tracksuit after a stocktake day), and he was generally a good role model for a young buffoon. He left and asked me to follow him. That was a no-brainer. In my second nightclub job at The Cuckoo Club (where I stayed for six years), I remember going to the first pre-opening meeting with all the bar staff. Going there I felt like I was a shit-hot bartender and knew everything there is to know; I had been hand-picked. Before the meeting, the bar manager had sent out a request to everyone to submit drinks to be shortlisted for the cocktail menu. I sent my best and only one. I felt confident. At this meeting I met Andreas Jansson and we started talking.

He was a fellow Swede and a few years older than me. He had just been to Australia (other side of the world) and before that worked several years in London in private members' clubs. He started talking about how he liked to make drinks with different sugars and infusions and a lot of other avant-garde stuff. I was lost. I realised I probably wasn't the hotshot I thought I was. My drink didn't make the cocktail menu. Andreas soon became bar manager and I hung on every word he said until it was time to cut the cord.

Eventually I devised my own style. In January 2012 I opened my own restaurant and bar in London, Dabbous and Oskar's Bar, together with Ollie. The aim was to have a neighbourhood restaurant and bar that overdelivered on food and drinks, served in an unpretentious setting with a lively atmosphere. No waiter hanging over you topping up your wine glass as soon as you have a sip, and music loud enough that you can fart without everyone hearing it. Everyone is welcome! Most of all, I wanted to serve the drinks I like and think are good. I didn't want to ask anyone for permission to do everything I wanted to do. If things are going well, it's because of me and equally if things aren't going so well, I only have myself to look to. Having my own bar has given me the freedom to further explore drinks making. I have a set menu formula that I like to work

from. Always replace like for like so there is a balance between different styles, ie dry and strong, bitter and sweet, sweet and sour. These are fundamental combinations. It's the components that build these combinations that I have freedom with. With some sense this isn't too hard. There is no point trying to be different for the sake of being different. Parsnip goes with roast dinners, not with gin. Melon goes with gin. If you put things you actually think will taste nice together in the drink you have a greater chance of making a tasty cocktail. In general, my drinks are pretty easy on the palate, even the very strong ones. It should however be said that if you don't like melon, the drinks with melon probably aren't for you. Same goes for all other ingredients.

I have always preferred savoury things over sweet so it's natural that some of these elements have crept in to the cocktails. However, the longer I have worked I have realised sugar makes savoury even better. Take ketchup, for instance. I'm sure everybody agrees it's a savoury ingredient. You wouldn't have it on ice cream, but there is loads of sugar in there, it makes it taste good! There is no way of getting around it: things like salt and sugar enhance flavours. Chips and milkshake?!? Brilliant! A cocktail for me is never a healthy thing. It's something luxurious and indulgent. The interesting thing about a lot of ingredients that are considered savoury is that they completely change their flavour once sugar is added. Cucumber tastes like melon, beetroot becomes a fruity and earthy explosion, and herbs and spices are a great and simple way to add an agreeably long finish to a drink.

I see every spirit as an ingredient with a certain flavour. You pick one that goes with the rest of the flavours in the drink. In an ideal world you would look at a menu and go: I like kiwi, I like avocado. This should be a good drink. Not, I don't like gin, I won't like this. In a cocktail bar that has more original drinks than classics there is always a reason one spirit has been chosen to go in a drink over another. Have a little faith. Don't let the alcohol put you off. We spend a lot of time creating these drinks. No one likes lukewarm gin but a lot of people like a cool gin and tonic. It's the same with other spirits. It might not be your cup of tea as a shot at room temperature, but in a cocktail mixed with other ingredients you may find you actually like it.

A challenging difference between food and drinks is that people are a lot firmer with what they won't drink. You often hear "I don't drink tequila" or "I don't drink whisky." Usually for various reasons that have either been experienced in early teens or hammered in by parents. Gin is a depressant, bourbon makes you aggressive and tequila makes you crazy and pukey. As I see it anything in excess will make you do stupid things. No need to blame the alcohol.

I decided to make this book to show that with a little care and effort in the kitchen and in sourcing your ingredients, you can make your house party or Saturday night a very memorable and special one. Some of the drinks will take some time in the kitchen to prepare and some are straightforward. What they all have in common, apart from being tasty, is that they are not technically difficult to make.

It has also been an incredibly fun journey writing this book. It's certainly not normal to categorise drinks by ingredient as opposed to style and this has proved to be a challenge at times. I have come up with a lot of new drinks and I've also really enjoyed digging up old specs (industry chat for recipes) and trying to find them by remembering who was working with me when we listed that drink. Each cocktail for me has a personal memory attached to it and hopefully you can attach your own to them too.

Anyway, here are some drinks I made...

BASE

500ml/20 fl oz Water
500ml/20 fl oz Caster
    sugar

All the recipes in this book that call for sugar syrup use this basic recipe. It's easiest to make using volume (so use cups if it's easier): it's just equal parts water and sugar. The recipes for other syrups and infusions are dotted throughout the book, and they also use this base recipe unless otherwise stated. Sugar is essential in everything tasty you drink even if it's the smallest amount. It not only elevates other flavours but it also takes the edge off the alcohol in a spirit. Adding sugar to a cocktail doesn't automatically make it a sweet one; sugar is a component that helps balance bitterness, acidity and booziness.

Bring the water to boil in a pan. Add the sugar and give it a quick stir. Wait until dissolved. Cool it down and put it in a sterilised bottle. You can store this in the fridge for up to 3 months. As a rule, when a sugar is infused with a herb or something dried such as tea (as you go on to do later in the book), you can keep it for up to 2 weeks. Most syrups infused with fresh fruit have a tendency to start fermenting after only 1 week.

ASSEMBLE

A lot of the drinks in this book use small measures of things. The easiest way to be accurate with these is to buy a good jigger or measuring cup with markings for smaller measures. Don't be put off: there is a reason these quantities are small. Sometimes small things make a big difference.

There are various strainers out there, but the most versatile and easiest one to use is the hawthorne. It consists of a spring attached to a metal lid that makes it sit safely on top of the shaker so you can easily strain off larger bits of fruit and ice. When using herbs, you don't want them to get stuck in your teeth, so you can double strain using both a hawthorne and a small sieve/tea strainer.

Useful bits and pieces to have:

Juicer
Soda siphon
Bar spoon
Boston shaker
Hawthorne strainer
Fine sieve/chinois
Kitchen scales

SHAKE

Half of looking like a good bartender is being confident about what you do. If you shake a drink, shake it like you mean it. I know it can be awkward the first time, being on show and thinking everybody is looking at you, but do try. Practise in front of the mirror if you have to.

The ice is meant to go back and forth, not side to side. Put a bit of effort into it! It's not just for show. Shaking aerates, dilutes, mixes and makes all the difference to a drink. And the type of shaker and technique will give very different results in the appearance and texture of a cocktail, particularly those containing egg white (or the espresso martini, my nemesis). Reluctantly I have to admit tin-on-tin bostons are the best all-round shakers. I don't use them when I work because I have a memory like a goldfish and can't remember what I put in each one if I can't see them. So if you are the same as me, boston glasses will do too. They are cheap and durable and you can see what you put in the glass and how full it is. Another key thing when shaking a drink is to fill the shaker with as much ice as you can fit. This will make sure the drink gets as cold as possible and also has the correct dilution.

SERVE

The last thing to cover is how to actually serve the drink. And one of the best bits about creating drinks is to pick the glassware and the garnish.

Volume and style of drink decides glassware. Large volume means large glass and smaller volume means smaller glass. Some drinks I prefer straight-up – these are meant to be drunk while still cold so don't need to be served on ice. But some shorter, stronger, more alcohol-led drinks can sit on ice for a bit longer so the flavour will evolve as the ice melts and dilutes the cocktail. It's a nice touch to keep cocktail glasses in the freezer if you have space. Even if it's just for ten minutes, this will help keep the drink cool, and a frosted glass also looks great. There is no real right or wrong with any of this: just do what feels right.

With any garnish I like it to be relevant to the drink. If it's a twist, pick a citrus that most complements the flavour profile of the drink. If the cocktail contains a herb, it seems sensible to use the same for garnish, or at least one that goes well with the rest of the drink. Sometimes, though, you just want it to look pretty.

Garnishes aren't always necessary but they can have a big impact on the drinking experience. Both citrus twists and herbs can add to the overall taste and balance when you put your nose to the drink or take a sip; equally, sometimes you might think the drink is perfect without one so you don't want anything to interfere. A twist can be as elaborate or as simple as you like it to be. Either just use a potato peeler and get an authentic, raw-looking zest, or start cutting it and do extreme citrus origami. Both ways are fine and will smell exactly the same, but if you have time, extreme citrus origami is definitely more fun and looks better in pictures. For herbs just pick the prettiest sprigs and stick them in the glass. If I'm serving the drink with a straw, I like to group the garnishes around it to make it look like it all belongs together.

The question of which ice to use is decided by how juicy and intense the cocktail is. If it has an intense and tangy flavour with lots of sugar and citrus, it can benefit from crushed ice as this will melt and dilute the drink quicker. It will also make the drink much colder as the liquid has more contact with ice surface. I generally use cubes as most drinks are either shaken or stirred and will have already been diluted to the preferred strength. I also try to use fresh juices where possible. They're quick to make yourself and taste so much better.

Good luck and I hope you enjoy the drinks!

DISCLAIMER

All recipes in this book are guidelines. They are balanced to how I like them to taste. I realise people have different tastes. If you want something a little less sweet it is always easy to remove part of the syrup or liqueur content or (last resort) add more citrus to your own taste. To me there is nothing worse than too much sugar and citrus. It completely drowns out all other flavours. Start with taking away rather than adding. The US measures in this book (ounces and fluid ounces) have been rounded up to make them easy to follow – you might end up with slightly more liquid in each cocktail, but the proportions are all accurate.

I always aim to use good-value-for-money products. Some are interchangeable, others are not. I have tried not to mention too many brands, and most can be substituted for one of your preference; mine are recommendations, but I feel they enhance the drinks. That said, Martin Miller's gin is more than a recommendation. For certain drinks it's a must. It's a modern-style gin but with a solid, classic base, meaning juniper is still apparent, but there is also a more contemporary botanical in the form of cucumber. It adds a cool sweetness and fruitiness. It does make a difference and the drinks won't be the same without it. Believe me, you need a bottle. Wine-based products such as vermouths are also an exception. They are not as easy to substitute. There is no hiding it: I'm a sucker for all the Cocchi expressions. If they are available near you please do try to use them because they make an ordinary drink into something extraordinary.

There is a glossary on page 186 which gives a bit more information on some of the ingredients.

CUCUMBER

These days cucumber is a very common ingredient in cocktails and is so for a reason. It's such an easy thing to add to a drink to instantly make it taste incredibly bright. By putting just a slice of cucumber in the shaker when shaking a cocktail you add a huge amount of flavour: sweet, vivid and almost fruity. You can also juice it, or dice it and muddle it in the shaker with other ingredients. It has a really refreshing scent, so it's great for garnishing too. And cucumber has one more quite unusual property: if you list cucumber as an ingredient in a cocktail it will instantly be ordered more than any other drink on the menu. Elderflower has the same crowd-pleasing properties. So if you put them together you almost don't need any other drinks on offer. Cucumber pairs very well with floral ingredients (such as elderflower) and also herbs, citrus and white spirits.

DILLUSION

50ml/2 fl oz Gin
15ml/ ²/₃ fl oz Fresh lemon
   juice
12.5ml/ ½ fl oz
   Elderflower cordial
7ml/ ¼ fl oz Sugar syrup
10ml/ ⅓ fl oz Cucumber
   juice
1-3 Dill sprigs, according
   to taste

Cocktail glass
Dill sprig

I created this cocktail in 2005 at The Cuckoo Club and it has travelled with me. It has always been very popular. Some say a pinch of salt brings it all together but I prefer it without. If you can't be bothered to juice cucumber you can dice about 4cm/1 ½inch and muddle it before you add the rest of the ingredients. If you're making lots at once, I strongly suggest juicing as you'll have a sore forearm as well as head the morning after.

Add all the ingredients to a shaker and shake with cubed ice for 10 seconds. Double strain into a cocktail glass.

FIZZY RASCAL

50ml/2 fl oz Potato vodka
15ml/²⁄₃ fl oz Fresh lemon
 juice
15ml/²⁄₃ fl oz Elderflower
 cordial
25ml/1 fl oz Apple juice
1 Large or 2 small sage
 leaves
1 Slice cucumber
Prosecco, to top

Highball glass
Sage sprig

This is one of the most popular drinks I've ever put on a menu. It's always well received, and the potato vodka and sage help give it a long finish. Potato vodka tends to have more character and flavour than grain vodka: my favourite is Vestal. If you can't get hold of it though, any other vodka will do too.

Put all ingredients except the prosecco in a shaker and shake with cubed ice for 4 seconds. Strain into a highball glass filled with cubed ice and top with prosecco.

SCANDINAVIAN LEATHER

35ml/1½ fl oz Skåne
   Akvavit or similar (gin
   works too)
25ml/1 fl oz Cocchi
   Americano
10ml/⅓ fl oz Maraschino
15ml/⅔ fl oz Fresh lemon
   juice
5ml/1 tsp Sugar syrup
10ml/⅓ fl oz Cucumber
   juice

Cocktail glass
Cucumber rasher

This is a delicious cocktail that actually tastes more like watermelon than cucumber. The sweetness from the aromatic wine and the floral maraschino work well with the cucumber and completely transform it. I have given you the option to use either akvavit or gin in this cocktail, although I strongly champion akvavit, especially when it's made with fennel and caraway. It's such a straightforward flavour and sticks out just enough to make the cocktail interesting as well as tasty. Gin can be used too but has a tendency to disappear in the mix a bit.

Put all the ingredients in a shaker. Shake with cubed ice for 6 seconds. Double strain into a cocktail glass.

APPLE

Apple is one of nature's most versatile fruits. In my earlier drink-making days, apple juice was more often than not my go-to lengthener. It bolsters, dilutes alcohol and gives body without affecting the flavour of the rest of the drink too much. I like to use it with both bold, bulky flavours and lighter, floral ones. It seems to work with anything though, really, anything. It's also great in its enhanced form – booze – be it cider or brandy.

Maybe not known to everyone, it also has tremendous health benefits. For as long as I can remember my mother made all the children in our family eat an apple at the turn of new year in order to start January in good health. On New Year's Eve, just after midnight, she would ceremonially cut and hand out apple pieces to everyone round the table. When I became a teenager and started celebrating with my friends, I quickly realised this was not the custom in every Swedish family. At midnight, when I pulled out a supermarket bag with apples and started offering them to my friends, I got some strange looks. I then had to explain this custom to a bemused group of teenage boys. I don't think they've kept that tradition up since, even though I have.

MEADOWSWEET SYRUP

200ml/8 fl oz Sugar
  syrup
  see Base, p12
20g/ ¾ oz
  Meadowsweet

Meadowsweet is a small white wild flower that grows in damp conditions and benefits from being dried and made into a tea, or in this case a sugar syrup. If you're not the 'go pick it yourself and dry it' kind of person you can also find it online. Meadowsweet has a similar comforting flavour to camomile: it has a long, gentle herbal finish that cosies up with creamy flavours but also softens sharper additions such as green apples.

Bring the sugar syrup to a boil in a saucepan then turn the heat off. Add the meadowsweet before the syrup cools and let it infuse under cover for 24 hours. Pass through a chinois or fine sieve. Pour into sterilised bottles and keep in the fridge for up to 2 weeks.

BASIL FAWLTY

50ml/2 fl oz Gin
15ml/ ⅔ fl oz Fresh
   lemon juice
20ml/ ¾ fl oz
   Meadowsweet syrup
35ml/1½ fl oz Fresh
   green apple juice
8-10 Basil leaves

Highball glass
Basil sprig

This is a real
crowdpleaser: long
and super-fresh. The
meadowsweet gives the
drink a rounded flavour
and the basil brings a
pleasing pepperiness.
If you can't find
meadowsweet, camomile
will work as well. Use in
the same way, by infusing
the sugar syrup first.

Add all ingredients to a highball glass and
add crushed ice all the way to the top. Whisk
everything together until the basil is bruised
and the liquid is cold. Fill with more crushed ice.

COMBINE HARVESTER TDI

50ml/2 fl oz Cider
   brandy
20ml/ ¾ fl oz Cocchi
   Vermouth di Torino
15ml/ ⅔ fl oz Apricot
   brandy
3ml/scant tsp Fernet
   Branca

Cocktail glass
Orange twist

As you can see by the ingredients list this is quite a stiff drink. The apricot brandy adds a welcome fruitiness and stops it all from becoming too musky. Try to use a good-quality cider brandy or calvados as this makes all the difference.

Put all the ingredients in a mixing glass with cubed ice and stir for about 45 seconds or to taste, the longer you stir the more you dilute the drink. Strain into a cocktail glass.

BURT REYNOLDS

50ml/2 fl oz Johnnie
   Walker Black Label
   (or other slightly
   peaty whisky)
20ml/ ¾ fl oz Fresh
   lemon juice
10ml/ ⅓ fl oz Agave
   syrup (or honey or
   sugar syrup)
2 dashes Angostura
   bitters
1 Small egg white
English cider, to top

Half-pint dimple mug

A great and refreshing
long drink that tastes of
smoky apples. Use a fairly
robust, semi-dry cider,
otherwise the whisky will
drown it.

Put all ingredients except the cider in a
shaker. Shake with cubed ice for about 6
seconds. Strain the drink back into the shaker
and shake again without ice for about 6
seconds. Pour into the half-pint dimple mug
and top with cold cider.

SORREL LEAF

You can often find sorrel growing wild in your garden or in parks and alongside country roads. It has a high acid content and is on its own not very nice. Dip it in sugar though and you're on to a winner. Any edible leaf, herb or vegetable changes its flavour drastically once sugar is added. Sugar counteracts bitterness and amplifies other flavours you might not taste otherwise.

Here I've treated sorrel like lemon and made a kind of lemonade from it. Once diluted and sweetened, this tart leaf becomes an extremely refreshing drink that almost tastes like green apples, and I absolutely love the colour too. All the work in this chapter goes into making the sorrel juice. It's a bit fiddly at first but once you've done it a few times, and I'm sure you will, you will find it is straightforward and that the outcome is delicious.

LARDER
SORREL JUICE

30g/1¼ oz Baby leaf
  spinach
130g/5¼ oz Sorrel leaves
900ml/36 fl oz Water
50ml/2 fl oz Fresh lemon
  juice
150g/5¼ oz Caster sugar

Wash the spinach and sorrel leaves. Put all ingredients in a blender. Blend on high speed for 30 seconds. Pass through a chinois or fine sieve. Pour into sterilised bottles and keep in the fridge. It will lose colour throughout the first day but will taste good for three days.

THE OTHER SIDE

35ml/ 1 ½ fl oz Calvados
   or cider brandy
25ml/1 fl oz Sauvignon
   blanc
15ml/ ⅔ fl oz Fresh lemon
   juice
10ml/ ⅓ fl oz Sugar syrup
100ml/4 fl oz Sorrel juice

Highball glass
Mint sprig, flower

This is a crisp, healthy-tasting drink. Sorrel and apple brandy is a great combination and the white wine adds further zip. If you are only making a few cocktails you can have the remaining wine with dinner, so pick one you like.

Put all ingredients in a shaker and shake with cubed ice for 6 seconds. Strain into a highball filled with cubed ice.

BETTER SAFE THAN SORREL

35ml/ 1 ½ fl oz Gin
15ml/ ⅔ fl oz Pear liqueur
10ml/ ⅓ fl oz Fresh
   lemon juice
125ml/5 fl oz Sorrel juice

Highball glass
Pear fan, sorrel leaves

Here's another green one. Pear adds a floral bouquet to the drink, and gin is always a solid base.

Put all ingredients in a shaker and shake with cubed ice for 6 seconds. Strain into a highball glass filled with cubed ice.

SORREL SEEMS TO BE THE HARDEST WORD

40ml/1 ⅓ fl oz Pisco
10ml/ ⅓ fl oz Melon
  liqueur
10ml/ ⅓ fl oz Fresh
  lemon juice
125ml/5 fl oz Sorrel juice

Highball glass
Honeydew melon sliver,
  sorrel, flower

I'm pretty sure by now you've figured out that there is a pattern to these sorrel recipes: booze, flavour (liqueur or wine), citrus, sorrel juice. The actual drink-making is easy. With good things going into the drink it's hard not to make it taste good. Try one of mine and see if you like it. After that, experiment on your own and see if you can find your favourite combination.

Put all ingredients in a shaker and shake with cubed ice for 6 seconds. Strain into a highball glass filled with cubed ice.

NETTLE

Most people where I am from probably think of either 'itchy excruciating pain' or 'soup' whenever nettle gets mentioned. I first used nettle as an ingredient many years ago and made a syrup that was Hulkishly coloured and then very quickly turned brown. It tasted great actually, kind of minerally and 'green'. Unfortunately it was far too volatile for a lazy man like me to make every day. So I left it there. Years later this guy waltzes into my bar with a nettle cordial that is *so* tasty. He also says he knows me. This guy turns out to be married to one of my sister's old school friends and we had met briefly a few years earlier around Christmas when I was in my pyjamas. I probably didn't make the best first impression but at least I made one at all, and when he heard I had opened a bar he made his way there. We have established a good trading relationship over the years where he provides me with cordial in exchange for interesting bottles of booze. Matt Lisle has been kind enough to share his recipe here. I have used this ingredient in many drinks. The beauty of it – apart from its elegance and long shelf life – is also its hairiness (a sort of tingle in your throat when you drink it). It has a strong nettle flavour and is intense. If you put it in a non-alcoholic drink you almost think you're drinking alcohol. The making process is long but very rewarding.

LARDER
NETTLE CORDIAL

200g/8oz Wild nettle
  tops
500ml/20 fl oz Water
1kg/2 ½ lbs Caster sugar
40g/1²⁄₃oz Ascorbic or
  citric acid

Go pick 200g/8oz of wild nettle tops. Wear protective gear. Wash them in a salad spinner and put them in a bowl. In a pot, heat up the water, caster sugar and ascorbic acid while occasionally stirring. When it hits 60°C/140°F, take it off the heat and pour it over the nettles.

Keep it in the fridge and stir it once a day for seven days. Strain it through muslin then pour into a sterilised bottle. It keeps in the fridge for up to 8 weeks or even longer in the freezer.

TEQUILA MOCKINGBIRD

50ml/2 fl oz Blanco
   tequila
15ml/ ⅔ fl oz Noilly Prat
   Extra Dry vermouth
8ml/ ⅓ fl oz Pine syrup
   see Larder, p58
8ml/ ⅓ fl oz Nettle
   cordial
1ml/dash Chardonnay
   vinegar
1 Cucumber slice

Cocktail glass
Lime twist

For a stirred drink this is surprisingly light and brisk. It's completely clear but has so much flavour. The chardonnay vinegar gives it necessary acidity but be careful not to add too much. The longer you stir a drink the more you dilute it: the sweet spot for me is when there is no longer a burn from the alcohol but all the flavours are still clear and present. This is usually between 30-45 seconds, depending on how cold your ice is.

Put all ingredients in a mixing glass and fill it with cubed ice. Stir for 45-60 seconds depending on taste. Strain into a cocktail glass.

STING & THE POLICE

50ml/2 fl oz Scotch
whisky (for extra
enjoyment infuse a
bottle with 10g/ ¹/₃ oz
pink peppercorns for
3 days)
5ml/1 tsp Qi smoked
black tea liqueur (if not
available swap for Islay
whisky and add 25ml/
1 fl oz of breakfast tea)
15ml/ ²/₃ fl oz Fresh lemon
juice
15ml/ ²/₃ fl oz Nettle
cordial

Small goblet
Mint sprig, juniper berries

This has a smoky
whisky and tea flavour
with minerally nettle
undertones. Crack the
juniper berries with
your fingers to get
some fragrance out of
them before garnishing.
Together with the mint
they finish off this cocktail
delightfully.

Put all ingredients in a shaker and shake with
cubed ice for 4 seconds. Strain into a small
goblet filled with cubed ice.

NEW WAVE OF BRITISH HEAVY NETTLE

50ml/2 fl oz Gin
20ml/¾ fl oz Fresh
    lemon juice
20ml/¾ fl oz Nettle
    cordial
1 Small egg white
Soda, to top

Highball glass
Shiso, lemon twist

This drink really lets
the nettle cordial shine
through.

Put all ingredients in a shaker and shake
with cubed ice for 4 seconds. Strain the drink
back into the shaker and shake again without
ice for 6 seconds. This will give the finished
drink superior head and texture. Pour the drink
into a highball filled with cubed ice and top
with soda.

BERRIES

I realise there are other berry chapters in the book, but this chapter is dedicated to red berries, which are the type most people think of when anyone mentions berries.

You can get berries in supermarkets pretty much all year long but they never taste as good as they do in the summer, which is why I see berry drinks as seasonal. Personally I find crushing them gives both the best flavour and colour. The main objective of making a drink with berries is to make it taste undeniably of berries, by adding other ingredients that enhance and complement the flavours. Here are three that I like: two use hibiscus syrup, which really helps bring out the berry colour, and its flavour is impeccable too.

When I was 14 I worked as a strawberry plucker for two weeks in the summer – this gave me a lot of admiration for all berry pluckers out there. I was slower than everyone else, and the days seemed to never end. It is not well paid and there is nothing ergonomic about plucking berries on all fours. After these two weeks, however, I was the proud owner of a £100 moped so in the end I probably thought it was worth it. If there is a lesson here I guess it's this: if you want a £100 moped, pluck strawberries for two weeks.

LARDER
HIBISCUS SYRUP

30g/1¼oz Dried
 hibiscus flowers
200ml/8 fl oz Sugar
 syrup
 see Base, p12

Hibiscus is a large flower that comes in many different colours. The most commonly used is pink, which is sold in dried form. It's usually used to make tea, which has a deep red colour and a readily apparent acidity. Once you add sugar to the flowers you have a syrup that is both sweet and sour and beautiful in colour: great for cocktails!

Put the hibiscus flowers in a bowl. Bring the sugar syrup to boil in a pan. Pour the syrup over the dried hibiscus flowers. Let it cool down. Pass through a chinois and pour into a sterilised bottle. Keep in the fridge for up to 2 weeks.

LITTLE RED RIDING HOOD

50ml/2 fl oz Martin
   Miller's gin
15ml/ ⅔ fl oz Fresh lemon
   juice
30ml/1¼ fl oz Hibiscus
   syrup
2 Large or 4 small
   strawberries
3 Raspberries
Champagne, to top

Small goblet
Grapefruit twist, flower

When berries are
in season this is a
phenomenal cocktail.
Berries and champagne
is always a good idea.

Muddle the strawberries and raspberries
in the bottom of a shaker. Add all the other
ingredients except the champagne and
shake with cubed ice for 4 seconds. Double
strain into the serving glass and top with
champagne.

CURRANT AFFAIRS

45ml/1 ¾ fl oz Vodka
15ml/ ⅔ fl oz Mandarine
   Napoléon (or orange
   curaçao, Pierre Ferrand
   is good)
15ml/ ⅔ fl oz Fresh lemon
   juice
10ml/⅓ fl oz Sugar syrup
25ml/1 fl oz Guava juice
24 Redcurrants

Cocktail glass
Redcurrants

This is another highlight from my bar menu. The sharp redcurrants cut through all the sweet ingredients and make this drink quite spectacular.

Muddle the redcurrants in the bottom of a shaker. Add all the other ingredients and shake with cubed ice for 8 seconds. Double strain into a cocktail glass.

SEX PANTHER

25ml/1 fl oz Blanco tequila
25ml/1 fl oz Cognac
15ml/ ²/₃ fl oz Fresh lemon
juice
20ml/ ¾ fl oz Hibiscus
syrup
20ml/ ¾ fl oz Cranberry
juice
3 Strawberries
Tonic, to top

Highball glass
Mint sprig, grapefruit
swirls, cut strawberries
and mint. Flamboyant
rose water spray

This is a very pleasant drink. The cognac gives it a full flavour and the tequila is light and fragrant. The hibiscus boosts the colour and also adds to the floral notes. It looks like there are a lot of things in there, but they all live happily together. The rose water spray is really for show and is almost unnecessary, but pretty fun. Put some rose water in an atomiser (you can often find these in your local chemist) and spray flamboyantly over the drink.

Muddle the strawberries in the bottom of a shaker. Add all other ingredients except tonic and shake with cubed ice for 6 seconds. Double strain into a highball glass filled with cubed ice and top with tonic.

PINE

To me pine has always been associated with 'wunderbaums', or 'magic trees' as I believe they are called in English, and 'raggare', a type of people native to Sweden who typically live in small rural towns, and love 1950s American cars and sex in the back seats of them. They are big fans of wunderbaums, pine-scented ones in particular. For them it's the ideal ornament for the rear-view mirror.

In wunderbaum form pine is not for everyone; I have however discovered that when used in drinks and sourced from Douglas fir needles, pine is actually quite subtle and elegant. Every cocktail contains sugar in some form – that's why I like using a sweetener with flavour – and this is a great syrup recipe that gives an elegant pine flavour. If you don't live in the countryside and find it hard to locate Douglas fir, try to pick up a Christmas tree when it's the season and make the syrup then. You can also freeze the branches or sprigs and use them later in the year.

LARDER
PINE SYRUP

1.5l /60 fl oz Water
30ml/1 ¼ fl oz Fresh
 lemon juice
30ml/1 ¼ fl oz
 Chardonnay vinegar
1kg/2 ½ lbs Caster sugar
2.5g/ ¼ tsp Ascorbic
 acid
120g/4 ¾oz Douglas
 fir pine needles,
 stripped of the sprig or
 branch, and bruised

In a pan, bring everything except the pine to a
boil then remove from the heat. Add the pine.
Leave to infuse overnight, then strain the next day,
pushing hard on the pine to extract all the syrup.

SPINAL TAP

40ml/1²⁄₃ fl oz Old Tom
  gin
12.5ml/ ½ fl oz Fresh lime
  juice
17.5ml/ ²⁄₃ fl oz Pine syrup
35ml/1 ½ fl oz Aloe vera
  drink
Three-prong cucumber
  fan

Rocks glass

What I really like about
this one is that it is almost
colourless but packs so
much flavour. I know the
measurements look a bit
fiddly but it is a cocktail
I have made many times,
and these measurements
are the best ones.

Put the cucumber fan in the rocks glass
and fill the glass with cubed ice. Pour all
the ingredients in and stir for 30 seconds.
Add more ice cubes to make it look
presentable. Feel free to play around with
lime and pine syrup ratios if my ideal measures
aren't to your preference. This drink is great to
put in a punch bowl, or to prepare without
ice individually and store in the fridge until
your guests arrive.

NORWEGIAN WOOD

50ml/2 fl oz Gin
20ml/ ¾ fl oz Fresh
   lemon juice
25ml/1 fl oz Pine syrup
1 Small egg white
6 White grapes
1 Lovage sprig
Soda water, to top

Highball glass
Lemon slice, lovage sprig

A lot of strong flavours fighting it out here. The flavour of the grapes doesn't really come through but they add essential body. Without them the drink is too short, and it can become a bit watery if topped with too much soda.

Muddle the grapes and lovage in the bottom of a shaker. If you can't find lovage try parsley or celery or both. Add the rest of the ingredients. Shake with cubed ice for 4 seconds, then strain the drink back into the shaker and shake again without ice for 6 seconds. This will give the finished drink superior texture and head. Double strain into a highball glass filled with cubed ice and top with soda water.

RYE RYE RYE DELILAH

45ml/1 ¾ fl oz Vulson
   White Rhino Rye
15ml/ ⅔ fl oz Cocchi
   Americano
5ml/1 tsp Mastiha
15ml/ ⅔ fl oz Fresh lemon
   juice
20ml/ ¾ fl oz Pine syrup

Cocktail glass
Pine sprig

This is a sharp, grassy and aromatic cocktail. It uses mastiha, a sweet Greek liqueur made from the resin of the mastic tree. It has a vegetal flavour and a spicy finish. If you struggle to find Vulson you can substitute it for another white/unaged whiskey or moonshine. You're after the rawness and purity of an unaged grain spirit. Vulson is superb though, so it's worth trying to get it. It's great just mixed with Ting and a grapefruit slice.

Put all ingredients in shaker and shake with cubed ice for 8 seconds. Double strain into a cocktail glass.

PEAR

I love pears! They are sweet, juicy and floral. The pear flavour is great paired with both darker spirits such as cognac or whisky and lighter ones such as vodka or gin. There is an array of different pear liqueurs, brandies and other flavoured spirits available. You're not using a lot of it in each drink, so it's worth taking a bit of time researching to find a good one – it does make a difference. For these drinks I have used the Gabriel Boudier range of pear liqueurs, but there are many others that are good too and also many in smaller bottles.

There are also a lot of different pears that you can juice to get a fresher, more genuine pear flavour. The downside of juicing pears is that the juice oxidises and turns brown very quickly, so the drinks need to be made with it straight away after juicing. Once it's mixed with citrus, alcohol and sugar, the oxidation will slow down and it will maintain its colour for a little longer. For this reason I usually use a liqueur or a spirit in the bar for pear flavour, but I wouldn't hesitate one second to make it fresh for home use. Anything you don't use in the drink you can enjoy on its own. Only one of these drinks uses fresh pear juice, but it is well worth making it.

PEAR JUICE

Pears
Juicer

There are a lot of types of pears and most people have their favourite. Try different ones to get varying results in the drinks. A simple but very tasty pear juice drink would be to just serve it long with a brandy such as calvados or cognac and a squeeze of lemon. It loses colour after about a minute but tastes good for a day or so.

For the juice, pick a pear you like, wash it and take the core out. Put it in the juicer and press play. You get roughly 100ml/4oz of juice from one pear.

JOURNEY

40ml/1 ²/₃ fl oz Cognac
15ml/ ²/₃ fl oz Cocchi
  Americano
15ml/ ²/₃ fl oz Boudier
  Bernard Loiseau Pear
  & Bay leaf liqueur (or a
  poire william liqueur)
5ml/1 tsp Gammel
  Dansk

Cocktail glass
Fancy origami deluxe
  grapefruit twist

Quite a punchy drink.
The pear isn't shy
but is a harmonious
accompaniment to the
warmth of the cognac.
The Gammel Dansk (a
Danish bitter) adds a
spicy finish. If you don't
have any of that you can
replace it with Fernet
Branca, but if so only
use half the amount.
The longer you stir a drink
the more you dilute it.
Everyone likes theirs at
different strength.
A good guideline is 30-45
seconds.

Put all ingredients in a mixing glass and fill with
cubed ice. Stir for 30-60 seconds, depending
on how strong you like it.

COLONEL SANDERS

35ml/1½ fl oz Pear vodka
(Grey Goose is good)
20ml/¾ fl oz Fresh
lemon juice
15ml/⅔ fl oz Green
chartreuse
15ml/⅔ fl oz Poire
william liqueur
10ml/⅓ fl oz Sugar syrup
1 Small egg white
1 Small mint leaf

Cocktail glass
Mint sprig

The secret blend of
herbs and spices in green
chartreuse provides an
intriguing backdrop to
the pear, and the single
mint leaf gives it extra
vitality.

Put all ingredients in a shaker. Shake with
cubed ice for 6 seconds. Strain drink back
into shaker and shake again without ice
for 6 seconds for added texture. Double
strain into a cocktail glass.

WHY IS IT A PEAR WHEN YOU ONLY GET ONE?

35ml/1 ½ fl oz Pisco
25ml/1 fl oz Sauvignon
  blanc
10ml/ ⅓ fl oz Fresh
  lemon juice
10ml/ ⅓ fl oz Sugar syrup
150ml/6 fl oz Pear juice

Highball glass
Pear fan, shiso leaf

An incredibly tasty and bold drink. The pear juice is enhanced by the fragrant pisco. Juice the pears just before you add the juice to the shaker, as it oxidises within minutes of extraction. The lemon and alcohol will stop this happening, so the cocktail will look fresh throughout the time it takes to drink it.

Put all ingredients in a shaker and shake with cubed ice for 6 seconds. Strain into a highball glass filled with cubed ice.

PEA SHOOTS

There aren't many tastier things growing in the garden than fresh, raw sugar snaps. Most people know what a pea tastes like and for many it's a given on the dinner table when in season, but not everyone has had it in a drink. The best way to get maximum pea flavour out of peas is to use the shoots rather than the actual peas or pods. They have a vibrant and pea-y flavour with a slight bitterness that works really well in cocktails. It naturally pairs beautifully with gin, but also with other white spirits too. Another welcome bonus of using the shoots is that they give off a deep green colour. If you don't grow peas yourself you can often find shoots in well-stocked supermarkets. The three cocktails I have made here all use shoots, which are also beautiful to garnish with.

PEAS & MINT

35ml/1 ½ fl oz Gin
15ml/ ⅔ fl oz Cocchi
  Americano
15ml/ ⅔ fl oz Sugar syrup
15ml/ ⅔ fl oz Fresh lemon
  juice
1 Mint leaf
Handful pea shoots

Cocktail glass
Pea shoots, flower

A very classic
combination of flavours
but in a new form.
Does what it says.

Muddle mint and pea shoots in a shaker.
Add other ingredients and shake with cubed
ice for 10 seconds. Double strain into a
cocktail glass.

PEA & TONIC

50ml/2 fl oz Gin
15ml/ ²⁄₃ fl oz Fresh lemon juice
10ml/ ¹⁄₃ fl oz Sugar syrup
10 Fresh lemon verbena leaves
Handful of pea shoots
100ml/4 fl oz Tonic, to top

Highball glass
Pea shoots

This is essentially a beefed-up gin and tonic. Both lemon verbena and pea go well with gin and pairing it with tonic seems very natural. If you can't find fresh lemon verbena, it still tastes great without, just not *quite* as great.

Muddle the verbena and pea shoots in the bottom of a shaker. Add all other ingredients. Shake with cubed ice for 4 seconds and double strain into a highball filled with cubed ice. Top with tonic.

PEAS, LOVE & UNDERSTANDING

35ml/1½ fl oz Pisco
25ml/1 fl oz Sauvignon
   blanc
10ml/1/3 fl oz Fresh
   lemon juice
15ml/ ⅔ fl oz Sugar syrup
15ml/ ⅔ fl oz Aloe vera
   drink
Handful of pea shoots

Cocktail glass
Pea shoots, lemon
   twist

This tastes like drinking life: it's incredibly vivid and fragrant. The sauvignon blanc adds a welcome tartness while also providing subtle tropical notes that weave their way through the rest of the ingredients. Using wine as well as lemon juice for souring means you're adding flavour as well as acidity.

Muddle the pea shoots in the bottom of a shaker. Add all the other ingredients and shake with cubed ice for 10 seconds. Double strain into a cocktail glass.

PINEAPPLE

Associated with tiki, rum and the Caribbean, the pineapple has many other uses too. In Swedish cuisine, exotic ingredients were big in the 1970s and pineapple often had a starring role. Dishes such as 'pork chop Hawaii' and something called nasi goreng – not as you know it – both came with tinned pineapple and were introduced in this golden age of Swedish food history. Many of the dishes from this time miraculously survived all the way to the time when I was growing up. I hold them responsible for scarring generations of kids.

I prefer pineapple in cocktails and puddings. Pineapple is a natural partner to other tropical fruits, but also teams up well with nuts, spices and dairy. The easiest way to use it in drinks is to buy a carton of juice and mix it with whatever you want. A better way is to juice the fruit yourself. Just cut the skin off, chop it into small pieces and stick it in the juicer. It has a tendency to completely take over a drink and it can certainly take a lot of abuse and still stand up to other strong flavours. In two of these cocktails I have tried to tame it so it takes a more complementary role, and in the other I've let it be itself.

GRAPEFRUIT SYRUP

250ml/10 fl oz Sugar
   syrup
   see Base, p12
Zest of 1 pink grapefruit

Put all the ingredients in a saucepan and bring to a boil. Take it off the heat and let it cool down. Strain off the zest and keep in a sterilised bottle. Store in the fridge for up to 1 week.

PINEAPPLE & JASMINE SODA

For the tea:
500ml/20 fl oz Water
6g/3 tbsp Jasmine silver
   needle tea leaves

500ml/20 fl oz Fridge-
   cold jasmine silver
   needle tea
250ml/10 fl oz Fridge-
   cold pineapple juice

To make the tea, bring the water to boil in a saucepan. Pour into a teapot or other heat-resistant vessel and add the jasmine silver needle tea. Let it infuse for 5 minutes and strain off the tea. Let it cool down.

To make the soda, put the jasmine tea and pineapple juice in a soda siphon and charge with 2 CO_2 cartridges. Keep in the fridge for up to 5 days.

WRAY CHARLES

25ml/1 fl oz Wray &
    Nephew Overproof
    Rum
15ml/ ²/₃ fl oz Fresh lemon
    juice
15ml/ ²/₃ fl oz Tonka bean
    syrup
    see Larder, p164
35ml/1 ½ fl oz Pineapple
    juice

Cocktail glass
Pineapple leaf

This is where pineapple
heads home to the
Caribbean and becomes
what we all know it as.
It's a classic rum and
pineapple combo with
the addition of tonka
bean, which adds a
welcome spicy finish.

Put all ingredients in a shaker and shake
with cubed ice for 6 seconds. Double strain
into a cocktail glass.

PISCOTHEQUE

50ml/2 fl oz Pisco
25ml/1 fl oz Fresh lemon
  juice
35ml/1½ fl oz Grapefruit
  syrup
50ml/2 fl oz Double
  cream
1 Small egg white
Fridge-cold pineapple
  and jasmine soda from
  a siphon, to top

Highball glass
Dried grapefruit slice,
  jasmine

This drink is all about texture: extremely fluffy and both creamy and zesty. Jasmine tea dilutes the pineapple to make it less overpowering and it also leaves a lightly perfumed finish. The ingredients list here looks all kinds of wrong, but the finished cocktail is absolutely delicious. (Not one for the weight conscious.)

This drink will initially split before you shake it. That's normal. Shake all ingredients together without ice for 10 seconds to bind them. Open the shaker and pour the drink back into the base. Fill the shaker with cubed ice and shake for 4 seconds. Strain the drink into a 12.5oz frozen highball glass. Charge the drink with the pineapple and jasmine soda from the siphon – quite aggressively at first so that the two liquids mix together, then carefully to fill to the top. Let it go over the edge of the glass a little bit – it will keep a head for quite some time. To make dried grapefruit slices, cut the fruit thinly from top to bottom and leave them in an oven at the lowest temperature until they're dry.

MOUNTAIN DEWAR'S

50ml/2 fl oz Dewar's
   whisky or other non-
   peaty blend
25ml/1 fl oz Sauvignon
   blanc (NZ or another
   tropical-flavoured one)
15ml/ ⅔ fl oz Fresh lemon
   juice
15ml/ ⅔ fl oz Sugar syrup
20ml/ ¾ fl oz Pineapple
   juice
3 Sage leaves

Rocks glass
Sage sprig

A truly tasty cocktail.
Whisky and sage gives
it a bit of backbone and
it is softened by sweet
pineapple and fragrant
sauvignon blanc. The end
result is one of subtle but
distinct pineapple with an
easy sage finish.

Put all ingredients in a shaker and shake with
cubed ice for 6 seconds. Strain into a rocks
glass filled with cubed ice.

MARJORAM

Marjoram is part of the oregano family, similar in flavour but not as intense. It can taste a bit soapy if used too generously, so be careful.

Putting herbs in cocktails is a great way to add a natural and curious note at the end. In the perfect cocktail there is a beginning, a middle and an end. Different flavours have what I like to describe as 'taste times' – when each taste is the most apparent. Herbs, spices and bitterness usually become most apparent towards the end of the drink, acidity early on, and sweetness tends to make itself known throughout.

THE GRAPE GATSBY

50ml/2 fl oz Gin
20ml/ ¾ fl oz Sugar
  syrup
20ml/ ¾ fl oz Fresh
  lemon juice
1 Small egg white
3 Fresh marjoram sprigs
6 White grapes
Soda, to top

Highball glass
*Lemon slice, marjoram
  sprig*

This one is one of my
all-time favourites. With
just the right amount of
marjoram it is incredibly
invigorating and fragrant
and a great substitute for
a gin and tonic.

Pluck the leaves from the marjoram
stems. Muddle the grapes and marjoram
in the bottom of a shaker. Add all the other
ingredients. Shake with cubed ice for
4 seconds. Strain back into the shaker and
shake again without ice. Double strain into
a highball glass filled with cubed ice and
top with soda.

STRAWBERRY LEMONADE

500ml/20 fl oz Water
200ml/8 fl oz Strawberry
purée (Boiron is a good
brand)
50ml/2 fl oz Fresh lemon
juice
100ml/4 fl oz Sugar syrup
30g/1 1/4 fl oz Fresh lemon
verbena or 7g/3tbsp
dried lemon verbena
20g/3/4 oz Fresh
marjoram

A great-tasting strawberry lemonade enhanced by herbs. You can switch the strawberry for another fruit purée if you want something different. It can at times be tricky to source fresh lemon verbena, in which case dried can be used too. Fresh marjoram is essential.

Wash the lemon verbena and marjoram thoroughly and pick the leaves off the stems. Bring the water to the boil. Pour the hot water into a heat-resistant bowl and add the lemon verbena and the marjoram. Let it infuse for 10 minutes and strain the liquid off. Let the liquid cool down. Add all the other ingredients to 400ml/16oz of this liquid, put in a sterilised bottle and keep in the fridge.

Drink this on its own or with your spirit of choice. It's very tasty with gin or vodka: use 50ml/2 fl oz of alcohol to 200ml/8 fl oz lemonade, served over ice.

PHYSALIS SOUR

35ml/1½ fl oz Gin
25ml/1 fl oz Velvet
   falernum
15ml/ ⅔ fl oz Fresh lemon
   juice
20ml/ ¾ fl oz Orange
   juice
6 Physalis fruits
2 Fresh marjoram sprigs

Rocks glass
Physalis, marjoram

This cocktail has a distinct Christmassy flavour with orange and spices coming through from the velvet falernum. Velvet falernum is broadly speaking a sugar syrup, often rum based but sometimes non-alcoholic, made with lime, ginger, cloves and sometimes other spices. I use the John D Taylor's brand, which is the most common.

Muddle the physalis and marjoram in the bottom of a shaker. Add the rest of the ingredients. Shake for 6 seconds with cubed ice. Double strain into a rocks glass filled with cubed ice.

BANANA

I love banana in drinks. I do wonder why it has had so much undeserved abuse over the years. Maybe it comes from its association with baby food, or maybe it comes from that drunken night on a gaudy holiday island where the banana liqueur didn't improve things immediately and especially not the day after. The fact is banana has a lovely round flavour and if used in the right way it doesn't have to be tacky or kitsch. Or it could be both, in a good way. I think secretly it's everyone's guilty pleasure.

Apart from being delicious on pizza with curry powder (one of the only tasty results of the exotic-ingredient boom in '70s Swedish cuisine), it can be used as a liqueur in boozy stirred drinks where it gives a soft, even finish. Where it really shines, though, is in blended drinks: it adds a freshness and a fantastic gooey texture. One of my career highlights was when I had a party of thirty or so crazy Swedes all drinking beer with chasers of banana liqueur on the rocks for a whole night. It was a very bizarre sight but it sort of makes sense, truly, beer and banana go well together.

RUM DIRECTION

45ml/1 ¾ fl oz Mount Gay
  Black Barrel or other
  unsweetened, dark
  aged rum
15ml/ ⅔ fl oz Cocchi
  Vermouth Amaro
15ml/ ⅔ fl oz Banana
  liqueur (leave a cigar in
  the bottle for a week for
  extra punch!)
5ml/1 tsp Velvet
  falernum
2 dashes Angostura
  bitters

Rocks glass
Lime twist

Apart from the banana
liqueur, on paper this is a
pretty serious drink. The
banana brings it to life
with some fruit and leaves
a long, rounded finish. The
cigar adds a bit of spice
and a gentle burn.

Stir all ingredients with cubed ice in a mixing
glass for 30 seconds. Strain into a rocks glass
filled with ice.

BEER GRYLLS

25ml/1 fl oz White rum
35ml/1 ½ fl oz Banana
  liqueur
15ml/ ⅔ fl oz Fresh lime
  juice
5ml/1 tsp Honey syrup
  see Larder, p158
Wheat beer, to top (I use
  Einstök White Ale)

Half-pint dimple mug

Banana and beer is a great combination that has been used before. The beer is the vessel for the banana flavour, like the bread is in banana bread. This is light and clean but deceptively punchy. Like a shandy on steroids.

Put all the ingredients except the beer in a shaker and shake with cubed ice for 3 seconds. Strain into a half-pint dimple mug and top with white ale.

ADAM & EVE

35ml/1½ fl oz
  Diplomatico Añejo or
  other aged rum
200ml/8 fl oz Milk
40ml/1⅔ fl oz Sugar
  syrup
½ Banana
½ Fig leaf

*Poco grande or sundae
  glass*
Banana crisp

This is my favourite drink in the whole book. It's thick, luxurious and comforting. Banana gives it a rich texture and the fig leaf provides a light, bracing finish and a hint of coconut.

Blend all ingredients in a blender on high speed for 15 seconds. Add a small scoop of crushed ice and blend for 5 more seconds. The ice will melt and chill the drink. Pour the drink through a fine sieve directly into your serving glass to remove the bits of fig leaf.

RHUBARB

Rhubarb is one of my favourite ingredients. It's tart and fragrant. Historically rhubarb roots have been used in Italian amaro for over a hundred years, where it gives a distinct bitterness. In the rest of the world it's probably best known for being the ultimate crumble partner. The best way to harness the purest flavour is to make a syrup. In a pudding you would probably add things like ginger and vanilla, and there are lots of other creative flavour combinations too; for cocktails though you want the cleanest rhubarb flavour so you can make as many different drinks as possible with it. All you need is rhubarb, sugar and water. You can add any other flavours when you make the cocktail. The result is a liquid that is both sweet and sour. Perfect for drinks!

I've had a fascination with rhubarb ever since I was a kid and used to thieve it from the neighbour's garden and eat it raw. My criminal career came to an abrupt end when one day I was caught red-handed with a mouthful of rhubarb while trying to rip more out of the ground. I couldn't sleep for a week in fear of my parents finding out. To this day they have no idea about this incident and I thank the man that caught me for stopping me going down what could have been a very slippery slope.

LARDER
RHUBARB SYRUP

250ml/10 fl oz Water
1kg/2 ½ lbs Rhubarb
250g/10oz Caster sugar

Wash the rhubarb and cut into slices.
Put everything in a pan and bring to a simmer.
Simmer for about 15 minutes or until the
rhubarb is broken up. Take off the heat and
pass through a chinois. The leftover pulp
can be used in a crumble, which has been a
staple in our staff breakfast for many years.
Add some syrup to a glass of champagne for a
delicious cocktail. The syrup will vary in colour
from light pink to almost red depending on
the rhubarb. Store it in a sterilised bottle in the
fridge for up to 1 week or longer in the freezer.

LARDER
JASMINE SYRUP

200ml/8 fl oz Sugar
   syrup
   see Base, p12
10g/ ⅓ oz Jasmine silver
   needle tea leaves

Bring the sugar syrup to boil in a pan and pour
it over the jasmine tea. Leave to infuse and let
it cool down. Strain off the tea leaves and keep
in a sterilised bottle in the fridge for up to a week
or so.

DISCO RHUBARB

50ml/2 fl oz Skåne
   Akvavit
50ml/2 fl oz Rhubarb
   syrup
50ml/2 fl oz Cloudy apple
   juice

Highball glass
Mint sprig, grapefruit
   twist

This is in many ways the ultimate disco drink. You can pour all three ingredients at once when you work and just bounce from glass to glass. Despite how simple it looks on paper it is actually very elegant. The akvavit has a subtle fennel flavour which tastes good with the rhubarb, and the apple gives it the needed length: this is a drink that is more than the sum of its parts.

Put all ingredients in a highball glass. Fill with crushed ice and give a quick stir. Add more crushed ice.

IKEA SOURS

45ml/1 ¾ fl oz Skåne
  Akvavit
10ml/ ⅓ fl oz Mandarine
  Napoléon
15ml/ ⅔ fl oz Fresh lemon
  juice
20ml/ ¾ fl oz Rhubarb
  syrup
10ml/ ⅓ fl oz Jasmine
  syrup

Cocktail glass
Fancy origami grapefruit
  twist

This is really quite an elegant drink. A great option for the Cosmopolitan drinker: sharp and fragrant. You can taste all the flavours individually throughout a sip and it has a long finish.

Put all ingredients in a shaker and shake with cubed ice for 8 seconds. Double strain into a cocktail glass.

CONAN THE RHUBARBARIAN

45ml/1¾ fl oz Martin
   Miller's gin
25ml/1 fl oz Aperol
25ml/1 fl oz Rhubarb
   syrup

Cocktail glass
*Fancy grapefruit origami
   twist*

A stiffer one. This cocktail can be made with other gins but I have tried that, and it doesn't taste as nice. It is always worth buying a bottle of Martin Miller's gin. The bitter orange and rhubarb root flavours from the Aperol are a neat match for the rhubarb syrup, and the gin brings it all together in style. The more sugar and richness a drink has, the longer it can be stirred and diluted without losing too much flavour.

Put all ingredients in a mixing glass and fill with cubed ice. Stir for 45-60 seconds according to taste and strain into a cocktail glass.

GOOSEBERRY

Another classic crumble ingredient: it has a tart, colourful and interesting flavour that is hard to describe in any other way than 'gooseberry'. Like rhubarb, it has a real sharpness that stands out keenly in drinks. You can either use it raw, muddled into drinks for a deep gooseberry flavour, or you can make it into a jam. By doing this you add considerably to the shelf life, and the jam tastes great with cheese on toast or with crumble and custard. The sugar in the jam counters some of the acidity in the gooseberries, and when cooked the flavour becomes richer and softer but still retains its tanginess. Gooseberries have a quite intense flavour and as such they can be used successfully with any spirit. I have generally used the jam more for whiskey drinks as I find it has a comforting quality that works well with whiskey, but for a lighter drink any white spirit does the job. Herbs and apples are also good partners to gooseberry.

LARDER
GOOSEBERRY JAM

250ml/10 fl oz Water
1kg/2 ½ lbs Gooseberries
350g/14oz Caster sugar

Wash the fruit. Put all the ingredients in a pan and bring to a simmer. Simmer until the fruit is soft and starting to break up – about 30 minutes. Take off the heat and put into a sterilised jam jar. It's also suitable for freezing.

WINGMAN

50ml/2 fl oz White rum
10ml/ ⅓ fl oz Kaffir lime
  juice
25ml/1 fl oz Apple juice
50ml/2 fl oz Gooseberry
  jam

Cocktail glass
Mint sprig

This packs a lot of flavour. Kaffir lime juice has a strong, perfumed taste which teams up well with the gooseberry jam. Kaffir limes (to juice) can be tricky to get hold of at the best of times so if you can't find them you can use 15ml/ ⅔ fl oz regular lime juice and a couple of frozen kaffir lime leaves (not dried). It won't give exactly the same result but it will still make a very tasty drink.

Put all ingredients in a shaker and shake with cubed ice for 8 seconds. Double strain into a cocktail glass.

ANTHONY EDWARDS

50ml/2 fl oz Gin
10ml/⅓ fl oz Fresh
   lemon juice
25ml/1 fl oz Apple juice
50ml/2 fl oz Gooseberry
   jam
1 large handful Fresh
   chervil

Cocktail glass
Chervil

This is a beautifully tangy drink. Chervil and gooseberry linger on the finish.

Put all ingredients in a shaker and shake with cubed ice for 6 seconds. Double strain into a cocktail glass.

REINCARNATION OF ANTHONY EDWARDS

50ml/2 fl oz Bourbon
15ml/²⁄₃ fl oz Fresh lemon
  juice
25ml/1 fl oz Apple juice
50ml/2 fl oz Gooseberry
  jam
1 Mint leaf

Rocks glass
Mint, flowers

A lot of big and
comforting flavours here,
and the single mint leaf
makes it extra lively.

Put all ingredients in a shaker and shake
with cubed ice for 6 seconds. Strain into a
rocks glass filled with cubed ice.

SHISO

Shiso, or perilla, which is another name for it, has its home in Asia and is part of the mint family. It is not as high in menthol flavour though, and has more of a nutty, citrussy and fragrant profile. It's typically used in Asian cuisine and is also a great cocktail ingredient.

I tend to use the large green or purple leaves over the smaller ones in drinks; they are easier to extract flavour from. All of them make beautiful garnishes, and even if not used in the actual drink they add something with their fragrance when you take a sip from the glass.

THRILLER IN PERILLA

45ml/1 ¾ fl oz Martin
  Miller's gin
15ml/ ⅔ fl oz Violet
  liqueur
12.5ml/ ½ fl oz Fresh
  lemon juice
12.5ml/ ½ fl oz Sugar
  syrup
3 Perilla/green shiso
  leaves

Julep cup
Shiso leaf

This was the first ever
drink I made with shiso.
It does a great job to
highlight the leaf's
fragrance. When you have
a flavour you love in a
cocktail, it's desirable to
try to make that particular
ingredient shine: I think
this drink does just that.
The gin and the violet
are ideal companions
to the shiso, and the
whole drink is verdant
and incredibly tasty.

Put all the ingredients in the julep cup.
Fill with crushed ice. Churn with the end of
a bar spoon. Top with more crushed ice.

SHISO FINE

50ml/2 fl oz Blanco
  tequila
15ml/ ²/₃ fl oz Fresh lime
  juice
20ml/ ³/₄ fl oz Sugar
  syrup
20ml/ ³/₄ fl oz Celery juice
2 Shiso leaves
1 Cucumber slice

Wine glass
Shiso leaf, cucumber fan

On paper this looks like a salad, and we all know you don't make friends by serving salad. You do make friends by sharing tequila though, and with the addition of sugar the salad ingredients transform into something quite different. It ends up being a savoury but almost fruit-like concoction.

Add all ingredients to a shaker and shake with cubed ice for 6 seconds. Double strain into a wine glass with ice.

PISCO INFERNO

50ml/2 fl oz Pisco
15ml/²/₃ fl oz Fresh lemon
    juice
10ml/ ⅓ fl oz Honey
    syrup
    see Larder, p158
1 Nectarine
2 Shiso leaves

Cocktail glass
Nectarine fan

Nectarine is a lovely fruit when in season, and shiso and stone fruits in general is a great combination. The slight nuttiness of the leaf combines well with the juicy, sweet tanginess of peaches, nectarines and apricots.

Cut the nectarine in half, remove the stone, then cut into pieces. Muddle the nectarine and shiso in the bottom of a shaker. Add the other ingredients and shake with cubed ice for 10 seconds. Double strain into a glass.

GRAPES

Grapes are a bit like apples. Grapes come in different colours, like apples. They are great for making alcohol, like apples. Another thing they share with apples is the part they play in a cocktail. In pure grape form it's very hard to let the grape shine and be the star player, as it has quite a delicate flavour. It is, however (like an apple), a great addition. It's both sharp and sweet; it dilutes, adds volume and softens alcohol without making it bland.

I prefer using green grapes over red grapes. They are a little bit sharper and grassier in flavour, but mainly they don't affect the aesthetics of the drink. For this chapter I've only made one drink with actual grapes – the other two drinks are made with wine and grapes in distilled form. However there are several drinks in other sections of the book that use grapes in the same way.

LARDER
WINE SYRUP

700ml/28 fl oz Merlot
   wine
150g/6oz Caster sugar

Wine is acidic, so adding sugar and reducing
intensifies the flavours and gives you a sweet
and sour syrup. You can use any red wine for this
cocktail, but I've picked Merlot as I think it's the
best foil to the other ingredients. It's also good
on vanilla ice cream with strawberries.

This recipe makes about 350ml/14 fl oz.
Put both ingredients in a saucepan and simmer
for 45 minutes. Let the syrup cool down, pour
into a sterilised bottle and store in the fridge for
up to 2 weeks.

GRAPE BALLS OF FIRE

50ml/2 fl oz Grappa or
   pisco
10ml/⅓ fl oz Aperol
20ml/ ¾ fl oz Fresh
   lemon juice
15ml/ ⅔ fl oz Grapefruit
   syrup
15ml/ ⅔ fl oz Pineapple
   juice
   see Larder, p76
1 Small egg white

Cocktail glass
Peychaud's bitters on top

I love both grappa and pisco. They are great for making cocktails and their floral and citrussy attributes cut through most flavours. This one is tangy and tropical.

Add all ingredients to a shaker. Shake with cubed ice for 6 seconds. Strain back into shaker and discard the ice. Shake again for 6 seconds to create a super-fluffy texture.

ROOT OF ALL EVIL

50ml/2 fl oz 100% blue
agave blanco tequila
15ml/ ⅔ fl oz Fresh lime
juice
20ml/ ¾ fl oz Wine syrup
20ml/ ¾ fl oz Beetroot
juice
15ml/ ⅔ fl oz Orange
juice
3 Salt flakes

Rocks glass
Lime twist

This drink is rich and
earthy and the beetroot
leaves a lingering
finish. The wine syrup
is delicious and any left
over can be used with
desserts.

Put all the ingredients in a shaker. Shake with
cubed ice for 6 seconds and strain into a rocks
glass filled with cubed ice.

GONE IN 60 SECONDS

35ml/1½ fl oz White rum
20ml/¾ fl oz Velvet
   falernum
15ml/⅔ fl oz Manzanilla
   or other dry sherry
15ml/⅔ fl oz Fresh lime
   juice
1 Small egg white
6 White grapes

Rocks glass
Mint sprig, lime twist

This is delectable!
The limey notes in the
falernum are a perfect
partner to the dry sherry.

Put all the ingredients in a shaker and shake
with cubed ice for 6 seconds. Strain back
into shaker and discard the ice. Shake again
without ice for another 6 seconds for added
texture. Strain into a rocks glass filled with
cubed ice.

CONDENSED MILK

Condensed milk, or the sweetened condensed milk I use here, is milk that has had the water removed from it and sugar added. It's essentially a milk syrup that is virtually indestructible until the tin is opened, and even then it lasts up to three weeks.

Apart from having a thick gooey texture, being sweet and tasting of milk, it doesn't curdle so it's ideal to use with citrus juices when you want to add milky richness to a drink but still retain some acidity. Condensed milk mutes stronger drinks and leaves a lingeringly creamy and slightly nutty finish. Milk is one of my favourite drinks so this is a great ingredient for me. As it's condensed, so is the flavour, so to get milk flavour you don't have to add half a pint and end up diluting the whole drink.

KIWI AVOCADO PURÉE

50ml/2 fl oz Sugar syrup
  see Base, p12
15ml/ ²/₃ fl oz Fresh lime
  juice
150g/6oz Peeled
  avocado
50g/2oz Peeled kiwi

This is like a sweet and fruity guacamole.
The avocado gives the purée a luxurious texture
and mutes the sharp kiwi. It's important that the
avocado is ripe both for texture and flavour.

Put the sugar syrup and lime juice in a bowl.
Cut the avocado in half and take out the stone.
Remove the skin and put the flesh in the bowl.
Remove the skin from the kiwi and put it in the
same bowl. Mix all the ingredients with a hand
blender until smooth. Pass the purée through a
sieve using a muddler or spoon to make it even
smoother. It oxidises quickly: keep it in the fridge
for up to 2 days.

GRAPE EXPECTATIONS (ABRIDGED)

50ml/2 fl oz Cachaça
15ml/²/₃ fl oz Fresh lime
   juice
10ml/¹/₃ fl oz Sugar syrup
25ml/1 fl oz Sweetened
   condensed milk
6 Grapes
1 Lovage sprig (or use
   parsley)

Rocks glass
Lime twist, lovage sprig

This is like a powered-up
Norwegian Wood (see
p60). Cachaça has such
a strong vegetal flavour
that it needs something
properly pungent to cut
through it. Lovage does
this and the condensed
milk mellows everything
and ties the drink together.
This is a cocktail that is
both creamy and fresh.

Muddle the grapes and lovage in the bottom
of a shaker. Add the other ingredients and
shake with cubed ice for 6 seconds. Double
strain into a small highball or rocks glass filled
with crushed ice.

TWO TICKETS TO PARADISE

45ml/1 ¾ fl oz Olive
   oil gin, regular gin or
   cachaça
   see Larder, p138
10ml/⅓ fl oz Fresh lime
   juice
25ml/1 fl oz Sweetened
   condensed milk
50ml/2 fl oz Kiwi
   avocado purée

Rocks glass
Mint, lime twist

Spirits listed in preferred order: ideally use the olive oil gin, because it really adds to the drinking experience. It complements the other flavours something incredible, it's well worth making. I love the texture of this drink: the avocado and condensed milk collaboration is magical and the kiwi gives it a real lift and stops it becoming too rich.

Put all ingredients in a shaker and shake with cubed ice for 6 seconds. Strain into a rocks glass filled with crushed ice.

THE HAMMER OF THOR

35ml/1½ fl oz Skåne
   Akvavit
15ml/⅔ fl oz Wray &
   Nephew Overproof
   Rum
25ml/1 fl oz Banana
   liqueur
25ml/1 fl oz Double cream
25ml/1 fl oz Sweetened
   condensed milk
1 pinch Chinese five spice
Porter, to top

Pewter pint tankard
Mint sprig

Named after Swedish
heavyweight boxing
champion Ingemar
Johansson, this cocktail
really does pack a punch.
As odd as it sounds, the
porter lightens this drink
– the best way to describe
it is like a Bailey's for
grown-ups. It's incredibly
complex with all the
spices, and the banana
adds a rounded finish.

Put all ingredients except the porter in a pint
glass. Stir together with a few cubes of ice for
15 seconds. Fill the glass up with cubed ice and
top with porter. Give it another quick stir to
mix ingredients together and top with more
crushed or cubed ice.

MELON

Melon, or Melopepo in Latin, native to Africa and southwest Asia, is a key ingredient in the classic 'melon boat' hors d'oeuvre (quite possibly from that previously mentioned golden era of exotic foods in the '70s), which involves the assemblage of a melon wedge with a slice of ham in the shape of a sail, held with the aid of a toothpick. Melons are also pretty tasty in cocktails and in this case, more classy too. There are many different types of melons and all taste and look unique. I've picked three common ones here that are suited perfectly to their respective drinks.

Melons have their seasonal peak in the summer months and that's when you should use them. The easiest and best way to use them is to just dice them up, discard the skin and muddle them in the bottom of a shaker to extract all the juice. Melons are naturally floral and fragrant, and this can be enhanced in cocktails by adding ingredients that accentuate these qualities, such as honey, wine, rose or orange blossom water, and many other floral ingredients.

SAFFRON SYRUP

100ml/4 fl oz Sugar
  syrup
  see Base, p12
0.4g/healthy pinch
  Saffron (depending on
  how big your packet is,
  just use it all)

Saffron is an expensive spice, so to get the most flavour out of a small amount you can either infuse it in alcohol or make a sugar syrup with it. I've opted for the latter. This gives you an intense saffron flavour and a syrup that you won't have to use too much of per drink.

Bring the syrup to boil in a pan and add the saffron. Infuse for 24 hours then pass through a chinois or fine sieve. Pour into a sterilised bottle and keep in the fridge for up to 2 weeks.

MAGNA MELOPEPO

40ml/1 ²⁄₃ fl oz Gin
25ml/1 fl oz Monbazillac
 or other Sauternes-
 esque sweet wine
15ml/ ²⁄₃ fl oz Fresh lemon
 juice
10ml/ ¹⁄₃ fl oz Saffron
 syrup (not essential but
 tasty; use sugar syrup
 otherwise)
3 chunks Honeydew
 melon, approx 150g/6oz
1 Sage leaf

Cocktail glass
Sage, flower

Best drink in the book.

Muddle melon and sage in the bottom of a shaker. Add all other ingredients and shake with cubed ice for 6 seconds. Double strain into a cocktail glass.

GRANDIOR MELOPEPO

50ml/2 fl oz Gin
15ml/ ²/₃ fl oz Fresh lemon
    juice
10ml/ ¹/₃ fl oz Orgeat
25ml/1 fl oz Grapefruit
    juice
2ml/2 dashes Rose water
2 chunks Watermelon,
    approx 100g/4oz

Highball glass
Watermelon wedge,
    mint sprig

This tastes of watermelon and heaven. Rose water helps bring out the floral elements of watermelon and the orgeat gives the cocktail substance and a nutty finish. Goes down very easily.

Muddle the watermelon in the bottom of a shaker. Add all other ingredients and shake with cubed ice for 6 seconds. Double strain into a highball glass.

PARVUS MELOPEPO

35ml/1½ fl oz Mezcal
20ml/¾ fl oz Cocchi
   Americano
10ml/⅓ fl oz Fresh
   lemon juice
10ml/⅓ fl oz Honey
   syrup
2 chunks Cantaloupe
   melon, approx 100g/4oz
1 slice Red chilli

Cocktail glass
Sliver of cantaloupe
   melon

A smoky melon drink
with the addition of chilli,
which is in there more for
flavour than heat.

Muddle the cantaloupe melon in the bottom
of a shaker. When it is a juicy purée add the
slice of chilli and gently muddle a bit more.
Add the rest of the ingredients and shake with
cubed ice for 8 seconds. Double strain into a
cocktail glass.

TEA

I don't feel entirely right about writing anything about tea as I generally don't drink much of it. If I do it's usually really strong with lots of milk and sugar. But what I've realised over years of serving people cocktails is that there is no wrong way of drinking anything. Have it the way you like it.

My favourite way of drinking tea is with alcohol. I find sugar and alcohol brings out much more flavour and also makes tea more fun. You can also pair it with other things you think will go nicely, and all of a sudden there is an explosion of flavours.

Tea is easy to work with. You can make a hot infusion with it, steep it in booze or make a sugar syrup. Making hot tea is the cheapest and easiest way. The downside is that if you use too much of it in a drink it can easily become too weak and watery. Sugar syrup is also a very economical way to get it into a drink, the downside being it is very sweet and sometimes you want more tea flavour than sweetness. That leaves infusing it into alcohol – there is generally a larger measure of alcohol than sugar in cocktails. This way is more costly but can sometimes be the best route to get the end result you are looking for. Generally speaking, for lighter cocktails, teas or syrups are ideal, and for bolder ones infusing the spirit will be better. Experiment, then do what works best for you.

GREEN TEA SYRUP

10g/ ⅓ oz Green tea
  leaves
200ml/8 fl oz Sugar
  syrup
  see Base, p12

Put the tea leaves in a bowl. Bring the sugar syrup to boil in a pan. Pour the hot syrup over the tea and let it cool down. Once cool, strain the syrup off, pour it into a sterilised bottle and keep in the fridge for up to 2 weeks.

COCCHI VERMOUTH DI TORINO INFUSED WITH EARL GREY

150ml/6 fl oz Cocchi
  Vermouth di Torino
10g/ ⅓ oz Earl Grey tea
  leaves

Bring the Cocchi Vermouth di Torino to a boil in a saucepan and immediately take off the heat to avoid losing freshness and alcohol. Pour into a glass with the Earl Grey tea and let infuse for 10 minutes. Strain off the liquid, pour it into a sterilised bottle and store in the fridge – it keeps more or less forever.

COCCHI & BULLWINKLE

35ml/1½ fl oz Cocchi
   Vermouth di Torino
   infused with Earl Grey
25ml/1 fl oz Gin
10ml/⅓ fl oz Manzanilla
   sherry
10ml/⅓ fl oz Campari
2ml/2 dashes Islay whisky

Cocktail glass
Grapefruit or
   bergamot twist

A strong, bittersweet
cocktail with a clear hint
of peat to it.

Put all ingredients in a mixing glass and
fill with cubed ice. Stir for 30-45 seconds
depending on how strong you like it, it will
dilute as you stir. Strain into a cocktail glass.

CRIMSON TIDE

50ml/2 fl oz Gin
10ml/ 1/3 fl oz Apricot
  brandy
20ml/ 3/4 fl oz Fresh
  lemon juice
15ml/ 2/3 fl oz Sugar syrup
20ml/ 3/4 fl oz Marco Polo
  red tea, or other fruity
  red tea
2 Raspberries

*Small highball or rocks
  glass*
Mint, raspberry cut in half

The Marco Polo tea is fruity and tastes of raspberry, apricot and vanilla. These flavours are amplified here by actual raspberries and a bit of apricot brandy – the result is light, bright and fruity.

Put all ingredients in a shaker. Shake with cubed ice for 4 seconds. Double strain into a rocks glass or small highball.

GOODNESS GRACIOUS

60ml/2 ½ fl oz Cocchi
  Americano
15ml/ ⅔ fl oz Fresh lime
  juice
10ml/ ⅓ fl oz Green tea
  syrup
35ml/1 ½ fl oz Aloe vera
  drink
Prosecco, to top

Wine glass
Mint sprig, cucumber slice

An unbelievably tasty
spritz with a subtle green
tea finish.

Put all ingredients except the prosecco in
a wine glass. Fill the glass with cubed ice.
Stir for 4 seconds. Fill with more ice and
top with prosecco.

OLIVE OIL

Olive oil has a flavour and freshness that competes with and perfects the often stronger notes of alcohol. You can add flavour to alcohol from any fat, but through experimentation, not always successful, I have found that I prefer vegetable fats over animal fats in cocktails. Animal fats have a tendency to taste very heavy whereas vegetable fats taste light and 'green'. I like to use a fruity and not too bitter extra-virgin olive oil, and the best way to use it is as a base flavour mixed with gin. The olive oil adds sweetness, viscosity and the obvious olive oil taste to the gin. The beauty of this method is that you can take the flavour from any oil without the fat content, and it's easy to do. The end result is a gin that is truly versatile. You can use it either in a gin and tonic or you can make some lovely cocktails with it.

GIN WASHED WITH OLIVE OIL

700ml/28 fl oz Gin
(I use Martin Miller's
dry gin)
200ml/8 fl oz Extra-
virgin olive oil

Put both ingredients in a bowl with a large diameter. Keep the empty gin bottle. Leave for 6 hours to infuse. Put in the freezer until the oil has frozen completely. Take out of the freezer and lift off the frozen oil. Strain the remaining liquid through a muslin cloth to remove any small bits of frozen oil that remains. Pour back into the bottle – it keeps almost indefinitely. The leftover olive oil (now melted and gin flavoured), can be used in dressings or for anything else you would use olive oil for.

BAY LEAF SYRUP

500ml/20 fl oz Sugar
syrup
see Base, p12
20 Bay leaves

Simmer the bay leaves with the sugar syrup for 30 minutes. Strain off and keep in the fridge for up to 3 months.

A TASTE OF PARADISE

45ml/1¾ fl oz Olive oil gin
15ml/⅔ fl oz Cocchi
 Americano
15ml/⅔ fl oz Fresh lemon
 juice
5ml/1 tsp Bay leaf
 syrup
10ml/⅓ fl oz Elderflower
 cordial
1 Small egg white

Cocktail glass
Shiso leaf, cut julienne

This drink is alive and
full of what I like to call
grown-up fruit flavours:
something that tastes
fruity but isn't an actual
fruit, the kind of thing
you can't quite put your
finger on.

Put all ingredients in a shaker and shake hard
with cubed ice for 7 seconds. Strain the drink
back into the shaker and shake hard again
without ice for that extra-fluffy texture.
Pour it into the cocktail glass and garnish
with the shiso.

ANOTHER DAY IN PARADISE

45ml/1¾ fl oz Olive oil gin
35ml/1½ fl oz Cocchi
  Vermouth Amaro
5ml/1 tsp Bay leaf
  syrup

Cocktail glass
Lemon twist

Often it's hard to pick out distinct flavours from gin, or any spirit for that matter. Adding sugar to a spirit is a great way to enhance flavours. In this drink sugar is added in the form of bay leaf syrup. To balance it and make sure it doesn't end up a syrupy mess, you need something bitter with a bit of acidity too. Cocchi Vermouth Amaro does this perfectly. The result is similar to a Negroni but in a much lighter style. Again, heaps of grown-up fruit!

Add all ingredients to a mixing glass full of cubed ice and stir for around 45 seconds or to taste, it will dilute as you stir. Strain into a cocktail glass and garnish with a lemon twist.

PARADISE CITY

45ml/1 ¾ fl oz Olive oil gin
10ml/ ⅓ fl oz Aperol
10ml/ ⅓ fl oz Apricot
   brandy
17.5ml/ ⅔ fl oz Fresh
   lemon juice
10ml/ ⅓ fl oz Sugar syrup
1 Small egg white
3-4 Fresh marjoram
   leaves

Cocktail glass
Oregano, orange twist

Finally, a fruity cocktail! Apricot cuts through all the other flavours and the oregano adds freshness in the end.

Put all ingredients in a shaker and shake hard with cubed ice for 7 seconds. Strain the drink back into the shaker and discard the ice. Shake hard again without ice for that extra-fluffy texture. Pour it into the cocktail glass.

KIWI

Native to East Asia, this brown, rather large and hairy berry is another great cocktail ingredient. Mixed with certain things like milk, cachaça or overproof rum it almost tastes like banana, but mixed with most other things it keeps its pure kiwi flavour. The fruit itself can be firm and sharp or soft and sweet depending on ripeness. I prefer mine not to be overripe so it still retains some of its sharpness. This is good for cocktails, as we always add sugar to balance anyway. Its flesh is bright green and makes the drink exactly that too. It generally works really well with herbs, citrus and white spirits.

A FISTFUL OF DOLLARS

50ml/2 fl oz Cachaça
10ml/ ⅓ fl oz Fresh lime
  juice
20ml/ ¾ fl oz
  Meadowsweet syrup
  see Larder, p32
1 Kiwi

Cocktail glass
Chervil

A very enjoyable cocktail indeed with lots of strong flavours. The meadowsweet helps take the edge off all the acidity and leaves a lingering, soft finish.

Peel and cut the kiwi into quarters then muddle it in the bottom of a shaker. Add all the other ingredients and shake for 8 seconds with cubed ice. Double strain into a cocktail glass.

FOR A FEW DOLLARS MORE

50ml/2 fl oz Gin
15ml/ ⅔ fl oz Fresh lemon
  juice
15ml/ ⅔ fl oz Sugar syrup
50ml/2 fl oz Pear juice
1 Kiwi
3-5 Oregano leaves
Soda, to top

Highball glass
Oregano, lemon slice

A very sparky and rejuvenating cocktail that almost tastes like it's good for you. The pear softens the whole drink and leaves a perfumed finish.

Peel and cut the kiwi into quarters then muddle the kiwi and oregano in the bottom of a shaker. Add all other ingredients except the soda and shake for 4 seconds with cubed ice. Double strain into a highball glass filled with cubed ice. Top with soda.

THE GOOD, THE BAD & THE UGLY

50ml/2 fl oz Gin
20ml/ ¾ fl oz Fresh
   lemon juice
15ml/ ⅔ fl oz Orgeat
1 Small egg white
1 Kiwi
4 Mint leaves
Soda, to top

Highball glass
Mint, lemon twist

Kiwi finds a nutty companion in orgeat and is enlivened with a suggestion of mint in this effervescent number.

Muddle the kiwi and mint in the bottom of a shaker. Add all other ingredients except the soda and shake for 4 seconds with cubed ice. Double strain into a highball glass filled with cubed ice. Top with soda.

SLOEBERRIES

'Grape of the forest,' some call it. Eating a raw sloeberry does not taste very nice at all. It's tart, tannic and extremely unpleasant. However, making cordial or, in this case, a sloe gin, is very easy and makes it taste very pleasant. To make a sloe gin you extract all the flavour from the berries with the help of alcohol, sugar and time. You end up with a liquid that has a fantastic deep red/purple colour and you also get some of the tannins, which help a drink taste drier when it is in fact sweet. This sloe gin recipe is created for cocktails and as such it doesn't have any sugar added to it. You will add it when making the cocktail, and by not having sugar in the sloe gin it's easier to avoid ending up with a cocktail that is too sweet. My sloe gin recipe makes an infusion that is sharp and tannic with a scent of violets and sloes, with a wine-like, although considerably stronger, balance and finish. If you like to drink it on its own just add a bit of sugar syrup.

SLOE GIN

350g/14oz Sloes to
700ml/28 fl oz gin

Sloe gin benefits from being made slowly. The more patience you have with leaving the sloes in the gin the better the result. It's perfectly drinkable after 6 weeks but I would recommend a minimum of 3 months. Sloes are tough and they take a long time to break down. Once the flesh is separated from the stone, the gin starts taking on nutty notes from the stone. If, like me, you aren't very patient, you can always make multiple batches and leave one or more for a longer period of time.

Freeze the sloes for at least 72 hours to break the skin and the cells. Put everything in a sterilised jar. Leave for at least a year, ideally, or 3 months minimum, turning the jar every week. It keeps almost indefinitely.

SLOE GIN PUNCH

50ml/2 fl oz Sloe gin
10ml/ ⅓ fl oz Fresh
    lemon juice
10ml/ ⅓ fl oz Sugar syrup
15ml/ ⅔ fl oz Pink
    grapefruit juice
75ml/3 fl oz Ginger ale
1 Cucumber slice
4 Mint leaves

Wine glass
Mint, cucumber

This is a great party
cocktail. It's easy to
multiply or make in a
punch bowl, and it will
be loved by most people.
Like a wintry Pimm's.

Put the cucumber slice and the mint leaves
in a wine glass. Fill it with cubed ice. Add all
the other ingredients and stir for 8 seconds.
Add more cubed ice.

SLOE GIN MARTINEZ

50ml/2 fl oz Sloe gin
25ml/1 fl oz Cocchi
    Vermouth di Torino
10ml/ ⅓ fl oz Maraschino
10ml/ ⅓ fl oz Orange
    curaçao
2ml/2 dashes Campari

Cocktail glass
Lemon twist, orange twist

If you already know and
like the Martinez cocktail,
you will be pleasantly
surprised by this version.
The dry sloe gin adds
a welcome acidity that
helps balance the drink.

Put all the ingredients in a mixing glass.
Fill it with cubed ice and stir for 45-60
seconds. Strain into a cocktail glass.

SLOE & STEADY

50ml/2 fl oz Sloe gin
10ml/¹⁄₃ fl oz Aperol
5ml/1 tsp Violet liqueur
15ml/ ²⁄₃ fl oz Fresh lemon
  juice
20ml/ ³⁄₄ fl oz Sugar
  syrup
1 Small egg white

Cocktail glass
Flower

This is a very perfumed
drink that almost tastes
like sweets.

Put all the ingredients in a shaker and shake
with cubed ice for 8 seconds. Strain liquid
back into the shaker discarding the ice, and
shake for another 6 seconds, for added
texture. Double strain into a cocktail glass.

HONEY

Honey is the most obvious substitute for pure sugar in a cocktail. It's a sweetener with a flavour instead of just being sweet: Mother Nature's own sugar syrup. The best thing about it is that there are many different kinds and they all taste different. All the drinks in this book are made with acacia honey, which is an easy-to-find, mild variety that doesn't overpower anything. To earn bonus points, I encourage you to try the drinks in this chapter with different honeys using the same base recipe for the syrup. I often use manuka as I like the taste, and I've also heard it gives you superhuman powers. Manuka does have a much more intense flavour than acacia and tends to come through more obviously in cocktails.

Honey in general gives me a comforting feeling and I find it has a rich sweetness which is suited to darker, bolder spirits such as rye and bourbon. In this chapter all the honey cocktails are made with citrus: it's a well-tested combination that works. It's also worth trying honey in a stirred and more booze-heavy drink. The Old Fashioned cocktail is perfect for experimenting with different sweeteners. It's a basic drink with just booze, water, sugar and bitters, in which you can easily pick out the different components. If you like this kind of drink it's easy to swap out one ingredient for another and see if you can make it even more to your liking.

LARDER
HONEY SYRUP

50ml/2 fl oz Hot water
200g/8oz Acacia or
other honey

Mix together! Using honey in a syrup (rather than straight from a jar) means it will combine with and dissolve into a cocktail more easily. It will keep in the fridge for up to 1 week.

POOH SOURS

35ml/1½ fl oz Bourbon
15ml/ ⅔ fl oz Cocchi
 Americano
15ml/ ⅔ fl oz Fresh lemon
 juice
15ml/ ⅔ fl oz Honey
 syrup
25ml/1 fl oz Lemon
 verbena tea (optional,
 shake drink longer for
 more dilution if you're
 not using it)
1 Small egg white

Honey pot
Flower, orange blossom
 water spray

This drink helps elevate
the floral notes of the
honey. To make the
garnishing spray, buy a
atomiser/spray bottle at
your local chemist and fill
it with orange blossom
water. Give it a spritz
above the drink.

Put all the ingredients in a shaker and shake
with cubed ice for 6 seconds. Strain back into
the shaker, discard the ice, and shake again
without ice for 6 seconds. Pour into the honey
pot or pewter pint tankard to serve.

FLOWER POWER

35ml/1 ½ fl oz Cachaça
15ml/ ⅔ fl oz Umeshu
  plum sake
20ml/ ¾ fl oz Fresh lime
  juice
10ml/ ⅓ fl oz Honey
  syrup
3 Lavender sprigs
Egg white

Rocks glass
Lavender

Plum and honey is a natural pairing. This drink has many contradictions but the outcome is something that is floral, raw, vegetal and soft. Not usually words that go together.

Put all the ingredients in a shaker and shake with cubed ice for 8 seconds. Strain the liquid back into the shaker and discard the ice. Shake again without ice for 6 seconds and double strain into a rocks glass filled with cubed ice.

COMBINE HARVESTER

50ml/2 fl oz Cider brandy
   or calvados
10ml/⅓ fl oz Pedro
   Ximénez sherry
2.5ml/½ tsp Maraschino
15ml/⅔ fl oz Fresh lemon
   juice
10ml/⅓ fl oz Honey
   syrup
25ml/1 fl oz Apple juice

Cocktail glass
Cherry

Apple and honey feels like
a natural combination,
which is amplified by
the rich burnt flavour of
Pedro Ximénez sherry.

Put all the ingredients in a shaker and shake
with cubed ice for 8 seconds. Double strain
into a cocktail glass.

TONKA BEAN

Tonka beans are the seeds from the kumaru tree, native to central and north South America. To me they taste like a cross between vanilla, cinnamon and pistachio: they have the same lingering, soft finish. They're often used in desserts and also perfumes. I think they're a great cocktail ingredient too. They have a pretty bold flavour, so they tend to lend themselves to aged spirits with bigger flavour profiles such as whiskies, rums and cognacs. There is one tonka bean spirit which I am aware of and have tried: it is from Van Wees, a Dutch genever and liqueur producer. It's a neutral spirit infused with tonka beans and it works very well in cocktails, but can be difficult to source depending on where you live. I tend to make a syrup directly from tonka beans instead. It's easy to make and you can buy the beans online in small quantities.

TONKA BEAN SYRUP

200ml/8 fl oz Sugar
  syrup
10 Tonka beans
  see Base, p12

Grate the tonka beans into a pan with the sugar syrup. Bring to the boil and simmer for 5 minutes. Let it cool down and infuse for a minimum of 3 hours. Pass through a chinois or fine sieve to strain off the tonka bean bits. Pour the syrup into sterilised bottles and keep in the fridge for up to 2 weeks.

TONKA BEAN JULEP

50ml/2 fl oz Bourbon
   or rye whiskey
12.5ml/½ fl oz Tonka
   bean syrup
2 dashes Angostura
   bitters
10 Mint leaves

Julep cup
Mint

This is a twist on the classic Mint Julep. The mint lifts the tonka bean and whiskey and together this is pretty delicious. As the ice melts the flavour will develop further.

Put all the ingredients in a julep cup. Fill it with crushed ice. Churn with the bottom of a bar spoon for 6-10 seconds. Add more crushed ice.

DUTCH BREAKFAST

40ml/1 ²/₃ fl oz Genever
15ml/ ²/₃ fl oz Fresh lemon
   juice
10ml/ ¹/₃ fl oz Tonka bean
   syrup
1 tsp Orange marmalade
50-70ml/2 fl oz-2 ²/₃ fl oz
   Lager, to top

Rocks glass
Liquorice stick, orange
   twist

A profoundly orangey,
malty and comforting
cocktail.

Put all the ingredients except the lager in a
shaker and shake with cubed ice for 6 seconds.
Double strain into a rocks glass filled with
cubed ice. Top with lager.

THE FLIPSIDE

35ml/1½ fl oz Rye
  whiskey or bourbon
20ml/ ¾ fl oz Banana
  liqueur
15ml/ ⅔ fl oz Tonka bean
  syrup
2 dashes Angostura
  bitters
1 Egg yolk
100ml/4 fl oz Ale, to top

Flip glass
Grated tonka bean

A delicious flip. Tonka bean and banana taste like heaven together. A flip is probably one of the oldest of cocktails, with its roots all the way back in the 1600s. Supposedly, it used to be theatrically prepared in a large vessel filled with beer, spices, sugar and rum which were then plunged with a hot fire poker to heat it up, which made it fizz and invert/'flip' the sugars. The modern flip is usually served cold, and egg yolk found its way in there too.

Put all the ingredients except the ale in a shaker. Shake with cubed ice for 6 seconds. Strain into a flip glass and top with ale.

COCONUT

Processed coconut comes in many different forms: water, cream, flaked, toasted, milk and booze. Apart from tasting of coconut they have little in common. They all have different textures and levels of sweetness; some are liquid and some are solid. For these cocktails I have used liqueur, coconut water and coconut cream. Coconut liqueurs, like everything else, come in varying qualities. I have recommended one that I like but there are many others too that will be fine. Be aware though that all liqueurs have different sugar content, so you may have to add or remove some accordingly in the drink. Coconut cream is a sweet coconut paste that is often used in desserts and pastries – perfect for cocktails! Coconut liqueur is clear and won't discolour the drink whereas coconut cream will make it cloudy. They both have an intense coconut flavour and essentially do the same job, but coconut cream tends to taste more 'genuine', whereas coconut water has a much more subtle flavour with only a slight acidity and sweetness. I have created a few different kinds of drinks in this chapter too. One that is very traditional in its flavour profile but the coconut makes it a bit more fun and leaves a light finish. The other draws inspiration from rice pudding, which it seems I can't get enough of. It's quite rich, but also nutty and floral, and the rice adds a starchy finish to the drink.

LARDER
COCONUT WATER INFUSED WITH RICE

500ml/20 fl oz Coconut
   water
50ml/2 fl oz Fresh lime
   juice
200ml/8 fl oz Orgeat
250g/10oz Rice

By washing the rice in coconut water you remove the starch from the grains, and this adds a pleasant, ricy, dry end note to the drink. With some imagination, it tastes a bit like rice pudding. On its own this drink is not great, but in a cocktail it's really quite impressive.

Combine all ingredients in a pot and leave in the fridge for 6 hours minimum. Pass through a chinois or sieve and pour the liquid into sterilised bottles. Store in the frige and keep for about 3 days.

WHISKEY BUSINESS

50ml/2 fl oz Rye whiskey
15ml/ ²/₃ fl oz Cocchi
   Vermouth Amaro
15ml/ ²/₃ fl oz Woodstock
   20yo sweet wine (50/50
   Pedro Ximénez and
   white port works too;
   both wines keep in the
   fridge for ages)
8ml/ ¹/₃ fl oz Casa D'Aristi
   Kalani (or other coconut
   liqueur)
2ml/2 dashes Fernet
   Branca

Cocktail glass
Cocktail cherry

A slightly controversial mix of rye and coconut, but it definitely works! The sweet wine tastes somewhere in between a sweet sherry and a port, and can as such be substituted for these two. The Fernet Branca gives it the necessary dry and bitter finish.

Stir all ingredients in a mixing glass with cubed ice for 45-60 seconds depending on your preferred strength (it dilutes as you stir). Strain into a cocktail glass.

TROPIC THUNDER

50ml/2 fl oz Rum, any
  type
15ml/²⁄₃ fl oz Melon
  liqueur, green if possible
  but any is fine
20ml/³⁄₄ fl oz Fresh lime
  juice
75ml/3 fl oz Rubicon
  Guanabana (available
  in any well-stocked
  grocery shop)
15ml/²⁄₃ fl oz Coconut
  cream
2 Kaffir lime leaves

Tiki cup
Everything you got!

This drink came about
as I needed a rum-based
crowdpleaser drink on the
menu. It tastes like every
tropical fruit in one big
rum punch. Tasty, fun and
with a ridiculous garnish.

Put all ingredients in a shaker and shake with
cubed ice for 6 seconds. Double strain into
a tiki mug filled with cubed ice. Put a cap of
crushed ice on top to hold all of your garnishes.

RICE, RICE BABY

50ml/2 fl oz Pisco
75ml/3 fl oz Coconut
  water infused with rice
1 Shiso leaf
1 Egg white

Cocktail glass
Flower

Lovely fluffy texture and a rich sweetness. The rice adds a dry, cereally finish, without which the drink would just be *too* rich and sweet.

Shake all ingredients with cubed ice for 12 seconds. Strain back into the shaker and discard the ice. Shake for another 5 seconds without ice. Strain into a cocktail glass.

PLUM

Growing up in Linköping I would eat plums straight from the huge tree in our garden. It produced small, deep purple, incredibly flavoursome and juicy fruits. The neighbours had plum trees too but with yellow fruits. I prefer the taste of purple plums, but more often than not I would eat the neighbours' instead. It sounds like I grew up in paradise with all kinds of fruit trees growing everywhere for everyone to eat from for free! It was pretty sweet, or maybe my memories are a bit more idyllic than the reality.

There are many kinds of plums available, but all the recipes here are made with the normal purple/red plums. Plums are simple to use in drinks and can be used in different ways. They have a lot of juice, which is easy to extract by just cutting them up and muddling them in the shaker. The colour you get from the juice is beautiful too: pale orange and pink. When the fruit is infused in spirits its skin gives off a lot of colour – the resulting liquid becomes deep purple and the flavour almost wine-like. Plums work with both lighter spirits and bolder ones.

LARDER
FIG AND PLUM RUM

6 Plums
4 Figs
1 Bottle aged rum

Wash the fruit, cut it all up and put in a bowl with the rum. Leave in the fridge for 3-7 days, depending on how patient you are. Pass off the liquid through a sieve and press out the juice of the fruit through the mesh. Pour the liquid back into the bottle and store in the fridge. It keeps almost indefinitely.

In this recipe, the fruit soaks up some of the alcohol in the rum while giving up its own juice, lowering the final ABV and making it a little softer and easier on the palate. It's a delicious rum infusion that can be used in many rum-based cocktails. Try making a Daiquiri with it, for instance. Very tasty!

SUGAR PLUM FAIRY

45ml/1 ¾ fl oz Scotch whisky infused with pink peppercorns (leave a handful in a bottle for 4 days)
15ml/ ²/₃ fl oz White port
15ml/ ²/₃ fl oz Fresh lemon juice
15ml/ ²/₃ fl oz Orgeat
25ml/1 fl oz Cranberry juice
1 Plum
Soda, to top

Highball glass
Mint sprig, cinnamon bark

A very rich and juicy long drink. The big and comforting flavours are perfect for the colder part of the year.

Muddle the plum in the bottom of a shaker. Add all the other ingredients except the soda. Shake with cubed ice for 4 seconds. Strain into a highball full of cubed ice and top with soda.

PARUM PLUM PLUM PLUM

40ml/1 ²/₃ fl oz Rum
   infused with fig and
   plum
40ml/1 ²/₃ fl oz Cocchi
   Americano

Cocktail glass
*Twist of lemon (discard
   after twisting over the
   top of the drink)*

This is an elegant drink.
The figs and plums give
the rum both sweetness
and acidity and makes
it almost reminiscent of
a wine. This drink also
tastes great warm with
blanched almonds and
raisins – put a few in the
drink before serving and
scoop them out with a
spoon while drinking.
This is the way we drink
glögg, or mulled wine, in
Sweden.

Stir both ingredients with cubed ice in a mixing
glass for 45-60 seconds or to taste, it will dilute
as you stir. Strain into a cocktail glass.

TOM THUMB

35ml/1½ fl oz Pisco
35ml/1½ fl oz Cocchi
    Vermouth di Torino
15ml/⅔ fl oz Fresh lemon
    juice
15ml/⅔ fl oz Honey
    syrup
    see Larder, p158
1 Plum

Cocktail glass
Plum and knife handiwork

A floral and juicy little
number.

Muddle the plum in the bottom of a shaker.
Add all the other ingredients and shake
for 8 seconds with cubed ice. Strain into a
cocktail glass.

HOMEMADE TONIC WITH BERGAMOT AND JASMINE

750ml Water
125ml/5 fl oz Bergamot
  juice
30ml/1 ¼ fl oz Fresh lime
  juice
320g/12 ¾ oz Caster
  sugar
15g/ ½ oz Vitamin C
  powder (buy it online)
  for a sour/tart finish
8g/ ⅓ oz Quinine powder
  (buy it online)
Zest of 1 large bergamot
  or of 2 small
Zest of 1 ½ limes
Zest of ½ pink grapefruit
2 Lemongrass stalks,
  bashed and roughly
  chopped
30ml/1 ¼ fl oz Jasmine
  syrup
  see Larder, p94
Soda, to finish

What's the ultimate drink? G&T! Gin and tonic aren't as great on their own as they are together: they complete each other. Both ingredients should be equally good. Here's a bonus recipe.

Put all the ingredients except the jasmine syrup and soda in a large saucepan and simmer for around 30 minutes. Pass through a muslin cloth twice to remove the quinine powder. Add jasmine syrup. This cordial keeps for 3 weeks in the fridge and can be frozen. When it's time to use turn it into tonic, dilute with soda water, roughly 1 part cordial to 3 parts soda. This recipe is never exact so you may have to add a bit more jasmine syrup for sweetness in the end, but it's up to your own taste. This is not your regular tonic: it's packed full of flavour. You can use this as a base recipe and add and remove ingredients as you like. Bergamot has its peak from December to February and is hard or expensive to get hold of for the rest of the year.

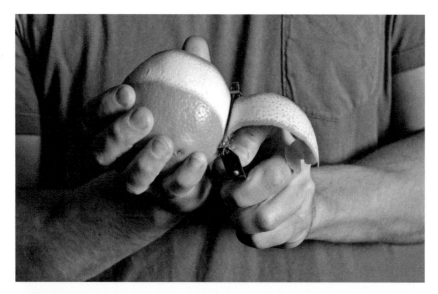

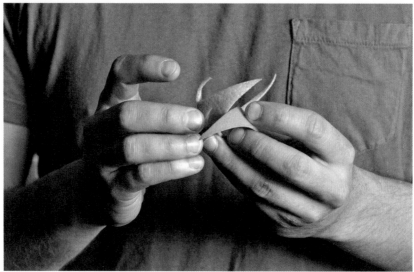

GLOSSARY

Agave syrup
Sweet syrup made from the Central and South American agave plant. Similar in appearance to honey but much sweeter.

Akvavit
Scandinavian neutral grain spirit flavoured with botanicals. It doesn't have as many botanicals as gin and usually doesn't contain juniper, the main flavouring in gin. Common additions are caraway, fennel and dill.

Amaro
Bittersweet Italian herbal liqueur.

Aperol
Bright orange, slightly bitter and sweet aperitif made with rhubarb and bitter oranges.

Ascorbic acid
Very sour white powder with a dry acidity, rather than the sweeter sort you'd get from a lemon.

Cachaça
Brazilian spirit made from sugarcane juice. A nice cachaça is verdant, creamy and spicy.

Campari
Deep red, extremely bitter Italian aperitif.

Chardonnay vinegar
Vinegar made from chardonnay grapes, a little bit softer than white wine vinegar.

Cider brandy
An appley, oaky distillate made from cider apples.

Cocchi Americano
Fortified aromatic wine from Piedmont in Italy. It doesn't contain wormwood so is not a vermouth. It's great to either drink on its own or in a spritz. My favourite way of using it is to put a splash in a cocktail. It ties all ingredients together. Like glue, but tastier. It also leaves a lingering satisfying finish.

Cocchi Vermouth Amaro
As the name suggests, halfway between vermouth and amaro. It has a prominent dose of quinine, which leaves a spicy bitter finish. It is partly made with barolo wine and is incredibly rich and moreish.

Cocchi Vermouth di Torino
My go-to sweet vermouth. Light, with a finish that just keeps on going – a great complement to bolder spirits and flavours.

Double strain
To strain your cocktail using both a hawthorne strainer and a small sieve/tea strainer.

Egg white
Added to cocktails for texture, but doesn't impact the flavour. You won't taste it.

Fernet Branca
An amaro from Italy: herbaceous, minty and highly bitter.

Gammel Dansk
Very bitter and spicy Danish bitter. On its own it's an acquired taste, but used in the right proportions in cocktails it's delicious.

Grappa
Grape distillate from Italy made from pomace – the leftovers of winemaking – as opposed to pisco, which is made from grape juice. It tastes like a rawer and beefed-up pisco.

Lemon verbena
Very fragrant herb that tastes like lemon.

Mandarine Napoléon
Mandarin liqueur.

Maraschino
Sweet liqueur that is distilled from the slightly sour marasca cherry. It's sweet and floral and a small amount makes a huge impact. It is also used to pickle cherries in, which are then used to garnish cocktails.

Mezcal
Mexican spirit made from agave. In essence a smoky rock 'n' roll version of its little sister tequila, with a less refined, purer flavour.

Muddle
To mush something up, ie fruit or veg. In this book it's always done in the shaker.

Orgeat
Syrup flavoured with almonds.

Pisco
Light, elegant, floral and citrussy grape distillate from Peru.

Twist
Made by cutting or peeling off a strip of zest from a citrus fruit. Its oils are squeezed over a drink for an instant hit on the nose.

Umeshu plum sake
Sake-based plum liqueur often sweetened with honey.

Vermouth
Fortified aromatic wine that crucially contains, among other herbs and spices, wormwood – a bitter shrub. There are two main categories: French and Italian. Broadly speaking, French is dry and Italian is sweet.

INDEX

INDEX

INDEX

ACKNOWLEDGEMENTS

Firstly a thank you to the key people who
have helped me realise this book:

Borra Garson DML
Zena Alkayat
Joakim Blockström
Glenn Howard
Euan Ferguson
All at Frances Lincoln
Julian & Gareth (for copious amounts
of glassware)

And also a very big thank you to friends
and family who have given me advice and
constructive feedback along the way.